YOUR WILL BE DONE

ORTHODOXY IN MISSION

Edited by
George Lemopoulos

TERTIOS
KATERINI

1989

WCC
GENEVA

YOUR WILL BE DONE
ORTHODOXY IN MISSION

CWME Consultation

of Eastern Orthodox and Oriental Orthodox Churches

Neapolis, Greece, April 16-24, 1988

Published
for the Commission on World Mission and Evangelism
by
WCC Publications, Geneva
Tertios, Katerini

ISBN: 2-8254-0951-0

Printed in Greece
by «TERTIOS»
Constantinos Papagiannoulis & Co.
Kolindrou 8
GR - 60100 Katerini
Emprimé en Grèce par: «Nea Stichiothetiki»
P. Giannoulis - K. Tsoleridis
6, rue Acheloou GR. 54627, tel. 031/542.940-522.503, Thessaloniki

The participants in the Consultation standing on the door steps of the Church of the Announciation, Evosmos.

Contents

Preface

At the Third General Assembly of the World Council of Churhes in New Delhi (1961), the majority of Orthodox opposed the merging of the World Council of Churches with the "International Missionary Council." As for the question of mission in non-Christian regions, the Orthodox did not feel it concerned them, nor that it was a chief priority in their ecumenical dealings.

Systematic opposition to this attitude came at that time from a group of young theologians, who set against it the clear concepts of Orthodox history, theology and worship. Members of this group began, as early as the first World Conference of the Commission on World Mission and Evangelism (Mexico 1963) to participate in the researches and efforts of the commission.

To assure a more sustained participation on the part of the Orthodox, a new post was created in 1970 in the then Division of World Mission and Evangelism, and the writer was called upon to head the office "for Research and Relations with Orthodox". One of the first long-term aims was the organization, with the participation of representatives of all the Orthodox churches, of a conference to examine the whole spectrum of the theme "Orthodoxy and Mission" in our times. A certain nonchalance on the part of the local churches caused the conference to be postponed. During the next fifteen years, through a series of Orthodox colloquies on specific themes organized by the Secretariat (headed from 1973 by Fr Ion Bria), it was possible to make progress on various aspects of the basic issue "Orthodoxy and Mission."

Within the framework of preparation for the World Mission Conference to be held in San Antonio 1989, a consultation was organized (coordinated by George Lemopoulos, the third secretary to date) at Neapolis near Thessaloniki (Greece) on the theme "Your will be done -- Orthodoxy in Mission." The consultation recapitulated the results of the spiritual stirrings in the Orthodox world at large during the last thirty years. Its main characteristics were: a systematic analysis of the contemporary situation of the Orthodox churches, the effort to become more sensitive to the messages of the times, a sincere self-examination, a theological study of the problem of mission, a sharpening of awareness of what the will of God is for the church of today, at the dawn of the third millenium A.D.

Avoiding any "unjustified embellishments," the members of the consultation attempted, through a careful study of the past and a lucid analysis of the present, to outline the appropriate "Orthodox" reactions to the new challenges of our times.

There was a common feeling that however much the missionary enthusiasm of the local churches had waned in the past the level of worship had been kept up, and so had fanned the spark of missionary awareness among the Orthodox. It was also felt that the sacramental life of Orthodoxy has direct social dimensions and missionary repercussions.

All the Orthodox bishoprics, synods and parishes need to awaken an urge for mission and to review missionary structures in view of the development of the modern world. The missionary life and structure of every parish is the key to a lively, contemporary Orthodoxy. It no longer appears strange -- as it did some decades ago -- to insist that the responsibility of every Orthodox Christian, whether on the parochial or the diocesan level, does not end at their geographical and cultural boundary. As members of larger groupings -- national, local church, etc. -- we are responsible for shortcomings in our love to less fortunate groupings, such as the peoples who do not know the gospel as they should, as a result of our mistakes and omissions.

Ecclesiologically speaking, there is no justification for polarization between internal and external mission. They are two sides of the same coin. The one should strengthen the other, should give it dynamism, prospects, maturity. There is but one mission of the church around the globe, today's megalopolis, with its rich suburbs (generally speaking, the lands of the north) and the poor, neglected neighbourhoods (generally speaking, the lands of the south).

Through the publication in this volume of the large majority of the presentations at the Neapolis Consultation, we hope that new opportunities will be given to Orthodox clergy, theologians and lay people of all ages to engage in theological research and missionary endeavours, with a view to fanning the flame of mission in the local churches. It is also hoped that a clearer picture will be given to the Christian world of contemporary missionary thought, questionings and self-awareness among the Orthodox.

Bishop Anastasios of Androussa,
Moderator of the Commission
on World Mission and Evangelism

Foreword

In the ecumenical world a major church meeting, even if at first glance limited to a particular confessional family of churches, is never an event totally isolated from other churches in the world. The Neapolis Consultation was no exception.

As Eastern Orthodox and Oriental Orthodox church leaders gathered to consider the nature and imperatives of Christan mission in our contemporary world, at the call of the Commission on World Mission and Evangelism (CWME) of the World Council of Churches (WCC), apart from a very small group of non-Orthodox observers it was a family gathering, worshipping, praying, debating and struggling together to articulate views on Christian mission that spring from age-old Orthodox faith, theology and experience. But also it was a consultation full of implications for non-Orthodox churches worldwide.

The forthcoming World Conference on Mission and Evangelism to be held in San Antonio, Texas, USA, in May 1989, offered a point of reference towards which the consultation could point. The conference will provide a place and opportunity for Orthodox churches to present their views on a world ecumenical stage, and the results of Neapolis will surely be in evidence there. Neapolis, however, was not limited to what might be presented at a particular ecumenical meeting. Often in the discussions what might or might not be presented to a world conference was forgotten, or at least seemed marginal to the discussions. More crucial were the deeper questions of what "mission" really means in Orthodoxy and how the historic Orthodox churches should engage in a mission in Christ's way within the complex daily history of today's generation.

By such an inquiry Orthodoxy was contributing not only to its own world of faith understanding but was also, as a part of the worldwide ecumenical Christian community, making its contribution to better Christian understandings across the earth. It is in the very nature of the ecumenical movement that all participants have the opportunity -- one might even say the right -- to both give and receive. Every sincerely held understanding of God's will for the world, however partial or even imperfect it may seem to us, deserves to be heard with respect by all. By the same token, all Christian communities, large or small, have the privilege of offering their convictions to the world. Giving and receiving, receiving and giving, are integral to the Christian experience.

Neapolis certainly gave much. The final document is already being read with much interest in churches and communities across the world that earlier had not known that the Neapolis Consultation took place. But it is also fair to say that the Neapolis discussion, far from taking place in a vacuum, received a great deal: the wisdom of early church fathers, the ecumenical discussions of recent years in which Orthodox and non-Orthodox have engaged, and the impact of the secular and technological world of our day.

The CWME considered it a great privilege to have a part in facilitating this event. The Commission itself must, and will, take the Neapolis document with utter seriousness. As the ecumenical community prepares for the coming world mission and evangelism conference, and for its follow-up beyond May 1989, the Neapolis contribution is a key one for Orthodox and non-Orthodox alike.

The CWME thanks God that in the process of preparation for the world conference, on the theme "Your Will Be Done -- Mission in Christ's Way," this particular Neapolis document has taken shape. Behind it are not only carefully considered ideas and reflections, theological wrestling and the effort to be faithful to Christian tradition and to the witness of the Scriptures, but also the personal experiences of many Orthodox leaders who in liturgy, prayer, study and life-struggle have endeavoured to give of their best. For all this, may God be praised!

Eugene L. Stockwell,
Director,
Commission on World Mission
and Evangelism,
World Council of Churches

Introduction

During the last fifteen years, the World Council of Churches' (WCC) Commission on World Mission and Evangelism (CWME) has organized Orthodox consultations and seminars on different missiological issues that were part of the ecumenical agenda. These consultations were hosted by Orthodox churches and communities in many countries. Their main purpose was to stimulate reflection among Orthodox theologians and church workers as well as to provide a ground for growing Orthodox participation in the missiological discussion of the Commission. At the same time, the reports and statements provided by these meetings contributed largely to the wider ecumenical debate, while the publication of their findings[1] enriched the international Orthodox bibliography in the field of mission and evangelism.

In the same spirit, more than sixty representatives of the Eastern Orthodox and the Oriental Orthodox churches, with God's grace and help and with the blessings and the encouragement of their spiritual leaders, met and worked together in Neapolis, Greece, from 16-24 April 1988, under the moderatorship of the Great Protopresbyter George Tsetsis, head of the delegation of the Ecumenical Patriarchate.

The purpose of this new CWME Orthodox consultation on mission was to enable the Orthodox churches to fully participate in the preparation, the event and the follow-up to the world conference that will take place in San Antonio, Texas (22 May - 1 June 1989).

Your will be done

This is a prayer and an invitation. A *prayer* that the will of God may be done on earth as it is in heaven. It reminds us that by asking for the justifying, sanctifying and liberating grace of God, we are called to faith, repentance (*metanoia*), discipline (*askesis*) and readiness to accept sacrifice, and even humiliation.

According to the patristic tradition, when we pray as the Lord taught us, we ask for the destruction of evil, the renewal of the world, the transfiguration of our being, the abolishment of the power of death, the supression of the sovereignity of sin, so that both in heaven and on earth there exists only one will, that of God. What we pray for is God's ceaseless intervention that his own will be done in us and in the world for the realization of our salvation and the coming of his kingdom.[2]

"Your will be done," is also an *invitation* to explore further what God's will means today in our personal lives, our witness, our communities and our churches. It suggests a mission in Christ's way, an involvement in the footsteps of the cloud of witnesses and martyrs who always struggled to be faithful and to maintain an authentic humanity.

In our task we are aware of God's promise, "I will put my spirit within you, and cause you to walk in my statutes and be careful to observe my ordinances" (Ez. 36:27). Thus, having received God's Spirit through our baptism and our participation in the holy sacraments, we know that God's will can be realized through our active involvement and participation in the church, our "*synergeia*" within the body of Christ.

This is both our mission and our communion with God's plan for the salvation of the world. The submission of our will to God's will, our obedience to his commandments, is in fact the restoration of our real freedom. Because when we repeat with St Paul "I live, yet no longer I but Christ who lives in me" (Gal. 3:20) and submit ourselves totally to God's will, by the assistance and the grace of the Spirit, our will becomes God's will and vice versa. This presupposes, therefore, that we must engage ourselves in self-criticism and self-knowledge, renew ourselves in repentance. And the result is not only a reawakening, but a profound crisis which provides a complete reorientation, a radical "change of mind," a deep change in attitude, an integral renewal that begins in our self-renounciation and is accomplished and sealed by the Spirit.

This very spiritual and existential struggle, apprehended and understood only in the living context of faith, which means a personal communion with the personal God, draws us to Christ's *kenosis.* Thus we discover that each of us, each community and the church is left in this world in its time, space and history, with a specific task: "to walk in the same way in which he walked" (I John 2:6).

Orthodoxy in mission today

The socio-economic, cultural, religious and political milieux in which Orthodox churches today bear witness to their faith are various, as are the challenges and questions put to these churches by recent developments in certain areas and certain situations.

Undeniably, their common task is "to testify to the gospel of the grace of God" (Acts 20:24) to all people. Orthodox churches aim to present to the world "the pure image" of Christ, to proclaim Christ not merely as he appears in the texts but as a living person. Do we at the same time, however, present his body, the church, not as an ideological system but as an existential reality of love, communion and renewal? How do our communities -- especially the parishes and the newly formed missionary communities -- challenge the surrounding secularized and divided world as "not-yet-community"? How do we live the joyful unity in Christ within our churches being challenged also by the awareness of the continuing division of Christians and the divisions of the world?

Life in Christ, life in the church, is salvation, communion with God, oneness, mission and evangelism. It is also a never-ending struggle for love and justice, for the perfection of the human being and improvement of the human family. How could we affirm today that these stages are in reality only one and the same movement, depending on the charismatic energy of the Holy Spirit? What is the intimate relation between our faith and our mission, between our vision of the world and our involvement in the world?

For the Orthodox churches the real force of renewal stems from the liturgical life and, especially, the sacramental experience. In the eucharist all humanity and all creation are united in the once-and-for-all offering of Christ himself. How is this sacramental life nurtured today in the midst of a broken and divided world? How have Orthodox churches lived and live their own sufferings as a sacramental experience, an authentic witness to the risen Lord, a mission in Christ's way?

Today's Orthodox presence on almost all continents, numerically small but strong in spiritual roots and rich in ecclesiological significance, tends to prove that the Orthodox churches have responded to the somehow "forgotten commandment."[3] How, in the life of the church, in its wholeness, does the missionary vocation become a major responsibility and concern? How does each parish and local community reveal its concern for the whole oikoumene, not only through prayer but also through a real mission involvement?

The consultation

In its effort to deepen some of these questions and to affirm that to speak of Christian witness today is, indeed, to speak of Christian life in all its dimensions, the consultation was rich in testimonies and experiences.

Participation in the life -- especially the liturgical life -- of the diocese and the parish was a deeply enriching and rewarding experience that brought delegates and local people closer together as brothers and sisters in Christ and allowed them to share in the joy of the resurrection that permiated the whole atmosphere.

Visits to the neighbouring dioceses, the Faculty of Theology, the Patriarchal Institute for Patristic Studies, the Minister of Macedonia-Thrace, the Mayor of Thessaloniki as well as Mount Athos offered the opportunity both to interpret the purposes of the consultation and to be informed of various visions and concerns at the local level.

Biblical reflections, papers and reports reflected the *martyria* of the Orthodox churches in their particular environments. Panel discussions widened the scope of witnessing with the testimonies of youth, women and clergy involved in missionary work. Broad and constructive discussions helped to deepen the calling to witness in the context in which each of the local Orthodox churches lives, as well as to become aware of the need for mission to those who have been deprived of the opportunity to hear the joyful and saving message of the Risen Lord.

Three important aspects of the consultation should be particularly noted:

First, the unfeigned love and generosity of our hosts in Neapolis. No one will forget the local hospitality as well as the continuous joyful presence of the youth. "Ascets of old and new times," the Rector of the Parish, Fr Alexander Kalpakidis, said, "used to kneel before their visitors. Why? In your faces, they like to say, we discern our Lord's face. 'If you see your brother or sister, you see God, your Lord.' Following this example, we also welcome you, kneeling before you, for in your faces we see our Lord and our gathering allows us to feel strongly the presence of the risen Lord among us and within us. Probably we do not speak your language. In our faces, however, as well as in our smiles, you shall discover our love and our joy to be your servants. During these days we shall try, above all, to speak the language of love." Likewise, nobody will forget all these people -- parish priests, university professors and students, lay persons -- coming to the meetings, asking questions, sharing concerns with the participants or joining their prayers with those of the consultation and thus making it both a "worshipping and learning" community.

Second, the collaboration and the discussions between the representatives of Eastern Orthodox and Oriental Orthodox churches became a hopeful sign for their further relations and for the success in their ongoing official bilateral theological dialogue. Having remained divided for fifteen centuries, Eastern and Oriental Orthodox churches march today, side by side, towards their unity. In spite of the difficulties, the whole atmosphere of the consultation helped the participants become more aware of their common ethos and spirituality, but also of the wall that separates them, compromising the authenticity of the message they bear within the difficult conditions of a profoundly suffering region. The consultation was a new opportunity to affirm the urgency to achieve full ecclesial unity in faith in order to face the challenges of the age and to proclaim that this unity is the source of salvation and the revivifying breath of the churches.

Third, the Neapolis Consultation will probably become a key event in the commencement of renewed Orthodox missiological thought and missionary practice. There is no doubt that mission and evangelism were on the agenda of several Orthodox meetings and gatherings organized by theological faculties, Syndesmos, local and regional bodies, the WCC as well as personal initiatives and efforts. Although the task of the consultation was a concrete one -- to prepare the Orthodox contribution to the San Antonio World Conference -- it was the first gathering of official church delegates from almost all Eastern and Oriental Orthodox churches to reflect on the missionary spirit and involvement of today's Orthodoxy.

The place

With the consent of the Holy Synod of the Orthodox Church of Greece and the kind hospitality of the Diocese of Neapolis and Stavroupolis, the consultation took place in Neapolis, a suburb of Thessaloniki, second town of the country and capital of northern Greece.

Only some kilometers from the historical centre of Thessaloniki, a town where the gospel was preached by St Paul some two thousand years ago, the Diocese of Neapolis and Stavroupolis and the parish of Evosmos helped us to become more aware of the fact that today, more than ever before, the church has to be involved in mission in Christ's way.

Next to the place where the two Epistles of St Paul to Thessalonians were received, the Diocese of Neapolis and Stavroupolis, since its creation in 1974, had to mobilize people to build more than fifteen new churches, to organize around them a strong parish life, to give priority to evangelization and Christian education, to take care of all those who have particular needs, and to participate actively in the development of the whole district. It is a district located between the cosmopolitan centre of the town and the industrial area, populated mainly by refugees arriving in Greece in the 1920s, facing serious problems of urbanization, secularism, search for identity; a district where spiritual, social, economic and ecological questions are of great importance.

Gathered in the parish Church of the Announciation, the participants had the opportunity to discover a modern "catacomb" -- the basement of the church -- where the liturgy is literally celebrated after the Liturgy in various ways. Inspired by the liturgical experience and functioning as a "parish centre," "spiritual home," "youth meeting point," "parish university," "restaurant of love" during great feasts and "open house" every day, this "catacomb" helped us to share the missionary zeal and the evangelistic witness of a vivid parish. It was a real pleasure to hear almost every day from the tireless youth of this small community the impressive missionary motto: "We are continously challenged to consider the whole world as our parish and not to limit ourselves to our parish believing it is the entire world."

The world calls us

There is no doubt that the great commission, the Lord's "Go, ye," remains the main impulse for mission. A contemporary Orthodox iconographer, however, interpreted St Paul's vision in Troas (cf. Acts 16 ff.) as complementary to it. In the first case Christ "sent" his apostles to the world. In the later case, the world itself "called" the apostles to help. Thus, the iconographer painted this vision as an ever-repeated call, addressed by the world to the apostles and the witnesses of Christ.

Our world -- depicts the iconographer[4] -- suffering from the consequences of technological domination over the human being, the emphasis of scientific and economic development over human values, the lack of faith and the silence of the churches, the secularization phenomenon, the non-respect of the creation, today puts its hope in the good news of salvation.

Carefully reading the same biblical passage, we could also discover a surprising contradiction that the iconographer has not been able to produce with his colours: the world that calls the apostles to help is the same world that persecutes and puts them in prison. Yet, it is always the same persecuting world which, in the person of the Macedonian prison guard, asks the anguishing question: "What can I do to be saved?" (Acts 17:30).

What is our message to this radically changing world that is full of contradictions? What would our attitude be towards this world where too many "strange gospels" are preached, each of them claiming total obedience and faithful submission? What is our real mission in this world where the root of tragedy probably does not lie in the fact that people lost hope and conviction but that they have never met Christ, or simply deserted him?

The Neapolis Consultation, I believe attempted, to repeat St Paul's answer to the above questions, to give the same message to the world: "Believe in the Lord and you will be saved, you and your household" (Acts 17:31).

Believe in the crucified and risen Lord!

> Christ conquered sin and death, reconciled and granted peace to all things on earth and in heaven (cf. Col. 1:20), and granted the joy and the hope of the resurrection which is the heart of the Christian message. 'If Christ be not raised, our faith is in vain; you are yet in your sins' (I Cor. 15:17).[5]

Christ is risen!

George Lemopoulos,
Secretary for
Orthodox studies and relationships,
CWME

NOTES

1. Ion Bria (ed.), *Go Forth in Peace, Orthodox Perspectives on Mission*, Geneva: WCC, 1986; George Tsetsis (ed.), *Orthodox Thought*, Geneva: WCC, 1983; Ion Bria (ed.), *Martyria, Mission, The Witness of the Orthodox Churches Today*, Geneva: WCC, 1980. It is appropriate to add that a considable number of Orthodox articles and studies on missiological issues are to be found in the *International Review of Mission*.

2. Petri Chrysologi, *Sermo 70*, P.L., 52,400.

3. The expression is borrowed from Bishop Anastasios of Androusa. Cf. Anastasios Yanoulatos, "The Forgotten Commandment," in *Porefthendes* 1 (1959), No. 1:1-5 and No. 2:3-5.

4. Frescoe in the narthex of St Paul's church at the Orthodox Centre, Chambésy, Geneva.

5. Final Report of the Consultation.

MESSAGES

AND

GREETINGS

Message from the Ecumenical Patriarch

Christ is risen!

We gladly take this opportunity to extend to the beloved members of the conference our greetings and best wishes for the happy outcome of its deliberations.

First of all, we wish to stress the fact that the aim of the World Council of Churches -- church unity -- is not separate from mission; for the evangelization of the world greatly depends upon the unity of all who believe in Christ as the Son of God and the Saviour.

Next, the theme of the conference, "Your will be done: Orthodoxy in mission," is bound to remind you all of its responsibility, as the one, holy, catholic and apostolic church of the creed, to contribute to the sacred task of bringing the saving truth of Christ to the two-thirds of the world's population who do not yet know him. "*All* the nations thou hast made shall come and bow down before thee, O Lord, and shall glorify thy name" (Psalm 86:9).

The truth of the gospel is not restricted to one nation, one place or one language. The eleven were sent forth on a universal mission to "*all* the nations" (Matt. 28:19). The Book of Revelation says of the Lamb that "he was slain, and redeemed us to God by his blood out of every kindred, and tongue, and people, and nation" (5:9).

Thus stress is to be laid on the necessity of mission, and the joint responsibility of all the churches to carry it out. The Ecumenical Patriarchate is concerned about a proper understanding and exercise of world mission. So we pray that the Lord may enlighten and strengthen you in the carrying out of his divine will. May his boundless mercy be upon you all.

April 12, 1988

Praying fervently to God
for all of you,

+ Dimitrios,
Archbishop of Constantinople,
New Rome, and Ecumenical Patriarch

Message from the Patriarch of Alexandria and all Africa

In the name of the holy, indivisible and consubstantial Trinity, it is my duty to thank the World Council of Churches (WCC) and congratulate the Commission on World Mission and Evangelism, which has summoned our Orthodox churches to this meeting "of one accord, in one place."

Our church feels that progress in mission, the commission to "teach all nations," is an obligation of the people of God. That means that Orthodoxy, united in its ranks, must nurture this progress with love and combine its forces to offer service and witness throughout the world, according to God's will. It also means that the collaboration of the Orthodox churches with the WCC for the smooth carrying out of our mission in Korea, India and Africa is a *sine qua non* condition.

Mission should help to unite the member churches of the WCC and the cause of charity in the freedom given by Christ -- a charity that does not divide by proselytization, prejudicial to the member churches and to the churches outside the WCC. I would like to believe, humbly and placing my trust in the Lord, that the days of sad division are over for good.

Our Patriarchate -- the church of the holy apostle and evangelist Mark -- humbly advancing in Africa from 1930, continues that course today in its provinces in east, central and west Africa. It is convinced it must give Christ crucified, dead and risen -- who signifies love, faith and hope -- to our African brothers and sisters. It must give them justice, freedom and unity without racial, cultural, political or social distinctions. It will continue this struggle with its feeble forces; that is why it seeks the cooperation of all and offers its own.

In its progress within its jurisdiction, i.e., Africa, our Patriarchate, thanks to the efforts of the late Patriarchs

Meletios II (1926-1935) and Christophoros II (1939-1967), has laid the foundations, in just a few years, of the African Orthodox Church. It is a small flock, with catechists, deacons, priests and bishops, all offspring of the African continent. It will carry on with the help of the Africans themselves.

I wish you success in your assembly. May God bless you and bestow on you all good things.

Christ is risen!

Easter Sunday, 1988

Praying to God for all of you,

+ Parthenios,
Patriarch of Alexandria
and all Africa

Message
from the Archbishop of Athens and all Greece

It is a great pleasure for me to welcome you, the members of the local Orthodox churches and venerable Ancient Oriental churches, to our country and its church.

You have come to Greece, to Thessaloniki, to consult among yourselves and to study the theme: "Your will be done," which is part of the theme of the World Conference of the World Council of Churches' Commission on World Mission and Evangelism to be held in San Antonio, Texas, during the summer of 1989.

Your task is an important one, for you are charged with the preparation of the Orthodox contribution to that conference. Conscious of the responsibility shouldered by those who possess the truth and the true faith, you are to give the Orthodox testimony on matters of mission and evangelism. You have come to formulate a joint reply to the questions of our times in accordance with the Lord's will, opening up your hearts to the illumination of his Spirit. In this way will your conference bear fruit to the glory of God.

Your presence in our country is an opportunity to familiarize yourselves with one of the most illustrious and historic of its cities -- Thessaloniki -- and its local church, which is a result of the missionary work of the great apostle of the nations, Paul, as well as the spiritual mother of the brother-saints Cyril and Methodius, who were born and raised in Thessaloniki and who, equal to the apostles, brought the gospel to the Slavs. Thessaloniki was also the home of a host of holy bishops, martyrs, confessors and ascetics.

The apostle Paul, called in a dream to travel to Macedonia to help its inhabitants enter into knowledge of the truth of God, obeyed his will and, armed solely with the enlightening, sanctifying and saving grace of the crucified and risen Lord, swept away the idols, overturned false deities, dispelled the darkness and established the religion of truth, love, goodness and salvation. He also laid the foundations of European and Christian civilization.

Eight centuries later, the brother-saints Cyril and Methodius, in response to the appeal of Rastislav, overlord of Moravia, journeyed to his country as teachers of the true faith in the vernacular. Taking up their cross of woes, persecutions and ill-treatment, the two missionaries, fired by their faith in God and love of their neighbour, bore the sacred flame of Christianity to those lands plunged "in darkness and the shadow of death." Moreover, they created a cultural movement that was to pave the way for the conversion of the Slavic peoples to Orthodoxy and their entrance into the family of civilized Christian nations.

This is all the more important inasmuch as this year we are celebrating the millenium of the baptizing of the people of Rus' in the waters of the River Dnieper for their salvation in Christ. Thus they reaped the invaluable harvest of the heritage of Cyril and Methodius. Fortified by their faith in Christ, they were to carry it beyond the Urals, as far as the Pacific Ocean.

The two saints of Thessaloniki, treading faithfully in the footsteps of St Paul, the founder of their church, blazed a trail for the mission of our church and charted its course up to the present day.

With these thoughts, I pray that the Lord may fortify you in your work; may he enlighten your hearts and minds with the eternal light of his resurrection so that you may debate among yourselves to his glory, for the spreading of the gospel message in the world of today, always bearing in mind the needs and anxious questionings of modern human beings, who so often stray far from God.

May the Lord pour abundant blessings on your efforts on behalf of his glory and the edification of the church, for the salvation of humankind, for which Christ died.

Praying to God for all of you,

+ Seraphim,
Archbishop of Athens and
all Greece

Greetings
of Prof. Dr Todor Sabev, Deputy General Secretary of the World Council of Churches and Staff Moderator of the Programme Unit on Faith and Witness

Eminences,
Graces and Excellences,
Distinguished Representatives of Church and State Authorities,
Very Reverend and Reverend Fathers,
Ladies and Gentlemen,

In the bright week after Pascha, when still in our churches are re-echoing solemn hymns of the Resurrection and our hearts brim with joy springing from the victory over death and evil, on behalf of the general secretary of the World Council of Churches I bring you festive Easter greetings: *Christ is Risen! Peace be with you!*

The Pascha period is the richest spiritual source of Christian zeal to witness to the Risen Lord and to proclaim the gospel to the ends of the earth (Matt. 28:19-20; Acts 1:8). Coming to this ancient city of Thessaloniki, we feel the missionary calling to follow in the footsteps of St Paul, Sts Cyril and Methodius and their disciples. Through this holy land of apostles and missionaries a great part of the world heard the good news. Faith and charity of Christians in Macedonia became a model for the whole church of Christ.

It is both symbolic and providential that our consultation takes place in this biblical city, which will give inspiration and blessings for a renewed commitment to and vision of the Orthodox understanding and priority of mission and evangelism today. After a series of over twenty-five Orthodox meetings and thirty publications by the World Council of Churches dedicated to missiology and spirituality, we are called to further reflection on the nature of mission in Christ's way today. Thus we seek to better serve the urgent need of our Orthodox churches and to provide a particular input to the forthcoming world mission conference and the World Council of Churches' Seventh Assembly. This should also open new ways for greater Orthodox involvement in missionary-ecumenical endeavours within the World Council of Churches and the total ecumenical movement.

Extremely vital are the topics that our consultation offers for discussion in a spirit of love and kindled in a specific context of life and witness of the Orthodox churches in the contemporary world. The major issues for consideration are:

> (a) theology of mission; (b) the role of the Orthodox churches in a secularized world, pluralistic western society, socialist context and call for "perestrojka," in a diaspora setting and in developing countries; (c) spiritual hunger in an Orthodox environment as a challenge and opportunity; (d) missionary dimension of worship and sacraments; (e) liturgical language, music and art; (f) gospel and culture today; (g) mission and social commitment; (h) interrelation between mission and unity, and between dialogue with living faiths and mission; (i) ecumenical dimension of mission; (j) common witness and rejection of proselytism; (k) united Orthodox efforts and shared resources for mission and evangelism.

The great experience of the participants at this consultation and the high quality of the hospitality provided by the local church will be conducive to the fulfilment of such an exciting agenda.

I would like also to assure you that the World Council of Churches will spare no efforts to accompany the realization of a vigorous Orthodox programme of renewal of mission for which you have the honour to be the architects and co-workers.

May I take this opportunity to express appreciation for your commitment to this noble task, as well as deep gratitude to the venerable Hellenic Church and its outstanding ecumenists, to the diocese of Neapolis and Stavroupolis, and personally to His Eminence Metropolitan Dionysios, to the state authorities, and to all those who are sustaining us with their prayers, who contribute to the fruitfulness of our meeting and who make memorable our stay in this lovely country.

Christ is risen!

Greetings from Mr Stylianos Papathemelis, Minister for Macedonia-Thrace

On behalf of the Greek government, it is my pleasure to greet this sacred gathering of persons, "come together in one place" to certify the substance and the responsibility of Orthodox mission in the world of today. I would say that the choice of site is a happy one, for greater Thessaloniki is the city to which, in the year 50 A.D., St Paul brought the message of salvation and the good news of the new teaching, new way of life and new creation. Thessaloniki -- the place where St Demetrius was martyred, and where his presence lingers. The place, finally, from which the two brothers, Sts Methodius and Cyril, set out on their great expedition to bring the light of the gospel to the Slavic peoples; today they are revered as protectors of Europe.

The timing of this consultation is well chosen. It is a time when that which we call "European alienation" or, in other words, the crisis of ideologies -- the deep and dramatic crisis of ideologies -- has led modern humanity into an impasse, especially the so-called "western man." This crisis of ideologies causes Europeans to be tossed about between nihilism and alienation. Their archetypes -- symbolized by Mephistopheles in Goethe's *Faust* as the expression of prosperity, the Great Inquisitor in Dostoyevski's *The Brothers Karamazov* as the expression of the demoniac, Don Juan (I would add) as the expression of sensuality -- those archetypes have worn thin and the word of Orthodoxy -- the incisive word of Orthodoxy -- needs to be heard in renewed and modern terms and broadcast in all directions, to all the points of the compass.

The remark that modern civilization has lost its ability to celebrate is common-place. We Orthodox may be proud of the fact that we still keep festivals and feast-days. We are always living celebrations, especially during these days of Holy Week and Easter. This voice of Orthodoxy, daily renewed in the worship of the Eastern Church, preserves, perpetuates and continually enriches the basic elements of human life: truth, freedom and beauty.

In a world constantly and now copiously changing, the message of "a change for the better" -- as St Gregory the Theologian expressed it in his exhortation -- as an essential message of Orthodoxy, must be heard. From this place -- or, more precisely, to the faithful of this city -- in the year 50 A.D., in the first Epistle of Paul to the Thessalonians, there were heard, for the first time, the great axioms of human civilization: "faith, hope and charity."

Through the work of your consultation, I hope that this message will be renewed for the world. I hope that the consultation will be a complete and utter success.

Address
of Metropolitan Dionysios of Neapolis and Stavroupolis

Christ is risen!

It is with the joy of the resurrection, along with honour and love, that we welcome you, dear fathers, brothers and sisters, representatives of the Orthodox and the venerable Ancient Oriental churches as well as the staff of the World Council of Churches (WCC), to our Diocese of Neapolis and Stavroupolis.

Both clergy and laity feel a special joy -- I would say the joy of a child, both in its purity and deepness. A joy that words cannot express. This joy stems from your presence here, in this humble section of the great and historical church in Macedonia, particularly in Thessaloniki. This church, which was planted by the apostle of the nations, St Paul, and watered by the blood of a cloud of martyrs, was protected and continues to be protected through the vigilance and ceaseless prayers of the neighbouring fathers of Mount Athos. Yes, brothers and sisters! We also are faithful and devoted children of this church who tirelessly cultivate and are being cultivated in the piety of the mystery of our faith.

Eminences,
Honorable Minister for Macedonia-Thrace,
Reverend Fathers,
Brothers and Sisters in Christ,

With the grace of God, the consultation organized by the Commission on World Mission and Evangelism of the WCC begins its work today in our diocese.

The presence amongst us of eminent brothers and sisters from all the corners of the earth, from the Orthodox churches of several countries having different socio-political and cultural contexts than ours, having different lifestyles and speaking other languages, gives us a foretaste of a "new" Pentecost before Pentecost. I would say that this presence is a holy and sacramental gathering. What deep and theological meaning is hidden behind the term "gathering"? "The grace of the Holy Spirit called us together," we sang some days ago in our churches. We are called and gathered so that we may be sent. Because the very notion of a gathering contains the following paradox: to gather and to commission.

As a movement, to gather contains the meaning of both to bring together and to send. So did the Lord who sent the gathered apostles to the ends of the earth. Thus, a gathering, every gathering of brothers and sisters in the name of Christ, either for prayer or participation in the holy sacraments, or for collaboration and mutual growth, has a deep and particular meaning in the life of the church.

At the same time, however, it becomes the starting point of our mission in the world, our journey and witness within the world, especially in the contemporary world. A world of pain and apostacy. This mission is unique because it seeks and heads towards salvation. Our world is full of dead ends. A way out cannot be seen. When facing the problems of the world, human beings experience dizziness and fear. Frightened and bewildered, they seek answers. These answers are found in the church. Precisely, the mission of the church is to provide an answer to this anguished question; to the tragic question of the Macedonian prison guard: "What must I do to be saved?" (Acts 16:30) and the answer is simple, as is the essence of the answering God: "Believe in the Lord Jesus, and you will be saved, you and your household" (Acts 16:31). Believe in him in whom "we have redemption through his blood, the forgiveness of our trespasses" (Eph. 1:7). This is the proclamation of the church. In this manner the church of Christ evangelizes. This, however, is not the only way of evangelizing. The church suffers with, is crucified with and feels the pain of every person created in the image of God.

Brothers and sisters in Christ!

How is it possible that our joy not be fulfilled? How could we not rejoice and be happy? How could we not be grateful that in our humble diocese, such an important and indescribable event, the event of Christ's tangible presence, is taking place? How can our hearts not be burning within us, and how could the doubt and incredibility of St Thomas the apostle influence us? We do not seek proof. Do not need evidence. We do not search for shelter. His presence is obvious. We live it. We need no one to attest if our hearts are glowing full of the light of his resurrection.

What we must do is be sensitive to the third bidding of that prayer, which he himself taught us: "Your will be done," and which so wisely became the theme of the present consultation. Yes, Lord! Your will be done!

How can we respond to this prayer? Have we remained on the level of using many words that bear no content and from which Christ wanted us to abstain? He taught us to pray. To ask for his grace and his help. He asked for our cooperation. He does not want our subjection as that of a slave. He asks for our voluntary submission to his will. His will, which is identified with the good. To this, God's will, we must show care, being sure that God's will could easily be done, because his grace is what makes us capable of wanting and doing it. "For God is at work in us, both to will and to work" (Phil. 2:13).

My brothers and sisters in Christ!

You have come from all over the world to bring us your desire for love. You have come to make us participants in your witness to the world which the love of God has commissioned you to serve. We embrace you with the love of Christ. Rest assured that we also attentively share in your concerns. How could we not? Your existential experiences are lived by us as well, and in our weaknesses strive so that the will of him who sent you to us be done.

In our region you will see the many places in which St Paul proclaimed the joyful message: Philippoi, Thessaloniki, Appolonia, Beroea and Methone. You will see the blood and relics of saints. You will see ancient and glorious churches -- which the piety of our fathers erected. We, today, continue their work. We are humble, few in number, rich in spite of our lack of riches and are debtors in fulfilling the will of God, thus facing many difficulties. We are attacked from all angles, even by those from whom support was expected.

We are not distressed, however. As much as we can, we place a small stone in the building of Christ's body. In our diocese, where his will commissioned us, we transform God's will, Christ's prayer "Your will be done," into action so long as our energies and Christ himself allow us. The priests of every parish, walking together, hand in hand with the faithful and being under the paternal supervision and guidance of their bishop, work towards the cultivation of the vineyard of the Lord. The bishop is a friend and a brother. Presiding, he assures and fulfills the unity in the bond of love and faith.

Moreover, the parish remains the nucleus and foundation of our daily Christian witness. Indeed, the gift that has been given to each faithful is offered for the cultivation of the small vineyard, the parish. If each of us could "repair his or her own municipal grounds" it would be a great blessing. Our witness, our struggle and our agony is that the intimate relationship in faith and love by all parishioners becomes a praxis, a daily experience and a way of life.

Our concern, our task, is to avoid living the faith as individuals in isolation. Our mission is to be gathered in the same place and sharing a common life so that the hearts and souls of our faithful may be one in the name of our Lord Jesus. Our task is to live the mystery of our communion with God and our fellow human beings. Pray that we may have a good account before the awesome judgement seat of Christ.

We do not know to what extent we are accomplishing our duties. In the few days that you will stay with us, we will seek your experiences and advice. We will ask your impressions, we shall try to benefit from you and your experiences in discovering new ways and paths. The intense beverage of the kingdom needs a sturdy recipient, perhaps a new one. We perhaps need new possibilities and ways with which we will offer it to the thirsty contemporary human beings.

Brothers and sisters in Christ!

Our joy of seeing you amongst us cannot be expressed in words. I would like to sincerely congratulate the WCC for taking the initiative for the present consultation and for its contribution towards the unity of the body of Christ.

I commend all of its members, who serve faithfully everywhere and especially those who work tirelessly in Geneva, offering daily the witness of our holy faith. Further, I thank all of you who came here without considering the costly effort.

We shall follow with much interest the procedures of your consultation. We know that you have a long way before you, which will lead you to the seventh General Assembly of the WCC in Australia.

We will remain here in these humble ramparts of the faith, though our thoughts along with our prayers will accompany you. We pray and shall continue to pray for you and your tasks, which are nothing but to serve God's will and work towards the unity of Christ's body.

May the Lord, the risen Lord, guide your steps, your reflections and your work in the pasture of salvation. Amen!

THE FINAL REPORT

I. WITNESSING IN THE OIKOUMENE TODAY

The apostolic witness

God offers salvation to all human beings of all eras without limitation or exception because God wants all to be saved and to come to the knowledge of truth (I Tim. 2:4). As a result of his unlimited love for humankind, which submitted to evil, distortion and death by abusing the free will, God sent his only begotten Son "that whoever believes in him should not perish but have eternal life" (John 3:16).

Christ conquered sin and death, reconciled and granted peace to all things on earth and in heaven (cf. Col. 1:20), and granted the joy and the hope of the resurrection, which is the heart of the Christian message. "If Christ be not raised, our faith is in vain; you are yet in your sins" (I Cor. 15:17).

Christ ordered his disciples and apostles to proclaim the good news of salvation to all nations (Matt. 28:19), to the whole world and to all of creation (Mark 16:15) so that the salvific grace of Christ should be revealed to all who "sit in the darkness and the shadow of death" (Luke 1:79). The apostles had to be and to become witnesses of all salvific events of Christ's life (cf. Luke 24:48; Acts 10:39). The apostles considered this very witness to be their main mission. In replacing Judas they elected someone who, like they, was a witness to Christ's resurrection (Acts 1:22). Preaching the resurrection, they assured all that they were its witnesses (Acts 3:16). They could not avoid the obligation to proclaim all that they had seen and all that they had heard (Acts 4:20) because the joy of such an experience is only "fulfilled" when it is shared and transmitted to others so that they also might become communicants and participants (I John 1:4).

Throughout the centuries, the Orthodox Church had offered its apostolic witness to the crucified, buried and resurrected

Christ. This same witness is continued by Christian mission today in the midst of such challenging conditions as secularization, pluralism, dialogue with other faiths and ideologies.

Witness in a secular world

The mission of the church has cosmic dimensions. Its aim is to embrace and to renew the whole world, to transfigure it into God's kingdom. Mission is to approach and draw near, to sanctify and to renew the world, to give new content to old ways of life, to accept local cultures and their ways of expression that do not contradict the Christian faith, transforming them into means of salvation.

During the first centuries of its existence, the church managed to transfigure the face of the oikoumene in spite of resistance by the world, which attempted to make the church conform to the world. The church responded to these tendencies towards secularization by entering into dialogue with Greek philosophy and pagan culture, which resulted in the production of creative theological patristic literature, the intensification of the ascetic elements of the Christian life of its communities and monasteries as a new means of martyria, and the expanding and enriching of its worship. Within the boundaries of liturgical life the church sanctified the activities and creative talents of human beings in all forms of art (literature, achitecture, painting, music).

In Orthodox worship the Christian message is proclaimed through all the senses. The entire human being participates with soul and body, mind and heart; hearing, smelling and touching. The icons, incense, the embrace of peace, the partaking of the eucharistic bread and wine enrich and fulfil the teaching and the preaching.

Education is more successful when influenced by the good news of salvation and a life in Christ in which the principle components are asceticism and eschatological expectation. Ascesis, as a voluntary withdrawal from a consumerist enjoyment of material goods, together with the desire to offer these goods to the poor and the needy, makes the passion and the cross of Christ more conscious in the life of Christians.

Mission is closely related to ascesis. For example, the Thessalonian Saints, Cyril and Methodius, before departing for Moravia, planned their missionary programme and prepared themselves in a monastery of Olympos in Bithinia. Their missionary team was composed of priests, deacons, monks and lay persons. From the Saints of the Oriental Orthodox Non-Chalcedonian family, seven monks left the monastery of St Minas in Egypt, formed a mission and evangelized Ireland. Their relics are still to be found in Belimina (near Belfast). Christian mission in Switzerland has been greatly affected by St Verena, from Egypt. In all Orthodox countries, monasteries assisted in the proclamation and witness of the Christian message.

Unfortunately, in recent centuries, especially following the Enlightenment and the French Revolution, the Christian message was gradually marginalized and humanism became an autonomous anthropology leading to atheism. In such a context, links with the church are severed and the principles of state ideologies and education, as well as consumerism, dominate, satisfying industrial ambitions both in the east and the west. Secularization torments Christian communities in the whole world because the task of different ideologies is to separate human beings from the influence of the church. This separation is caused by destructive forces against the church, thus diminishing the church's diakonia in the world.

Some, who are not satisfied with secularized society, turn not to Christianity but to eastern cults. Islam, in confronting secularization, often turns to a more conservative lifestyle; the reaction to western humanism sometimes leads to an extreme theocracy, which demeans the human being.

The abundance of material goods and economic conformism, dechristianized state power and education, the lack of Christian perspective in the mass-media, the weakness of the family in exercising Christian pedagogical work and the diminishing of the spiritual and apostolic role of motherhood leads to secularism. The contradiction between words and deeds in the life of Christians further contributes to the development of a secular way of life.

Nevertheless, many human beings continue to be attracted to Orthodox Christianity through its asceticism and mysticism, the joy of the resurrection in its worship, the presence of ascetics and saints, and the proof through holiness that Christians are not conformed to the world (cf. Rom. 12:2; I Pet. 1:14).

Witness within a pluralistic society and among believers of other faiths

Today, Christianity is in a situation similar to that of the apostolic era when it faced syncretism and different philosophies or religions. A pluralistic world brings Christianity into confrontation and dialogue with other teachings and faiths. Despite intolerance and fanaticism, Christians can use the immense potential offered by contemporary technology to witness to and evangelize others, to lead them in Christ's way. Christianity sees in a positive way the creative work of human beings when it leads to the uplifting of humanity and to the glory of God. To understand the cultural particularities of the evangelized, we must speak their language, respond with love to both spiritual and material deprivation and bring life and brilliance to each eucharistic community. The love we owe to those of other faiths makes more imperative our duty to confirm, as did the early Christian Apologists, whatever truth may be found in them while affirming the fullness and authenticity of the salvific truth of Christianity, even under pressure of persecution. The Orthodox churches, continuing the apostolic witness, have given tangible proof of endurance through the cloud of witnesses and new martyrs.

The awareness of the real needs of other people in this world helps us in the fulfilment of our missionary work and diakonia. Here, the basic missionary principle does nòt lose its eternal significance for a consistent and holy Christian life, which impresses and is beneficial to the awakening of those outside the church. In the midst of peoples and cultures where Christians live with all other persons, mission in Christ's way ought to lead towards sanctity of life, as an early Christian text of the second century states:

> Christians are not distinguished from others because of their homelands, their languages and their customs. Moreover, they do not live in separate towns, neither do they use a different dialect....However, while living in Greek and barbarian (non-Greek) cities, following the indigenous customs pertaining to clothing, food, and lifestyle, they provide an admirable and extraordinary way of life (Epistle to Diognetos, 5).

II. MISSION AND UNITY

Ecclesiological perspectives

The apostolic community was gathered into one body by the Holy Spirit in the power and joy of the resurrection (cf. John 20:22). Members of this community were called to be witnesses to the risen Christ "to the ends of the earth" (Acts 1:8). The ground of unity of the church, the body of Christ, is the love and unity eternally manifested in the life of the Holy Trinity. The church, as the presence of the kingdom of God, is called to manifest this trinitarian communion and love within its fold and towards the world. The church's mission is the expression of this unity and love.

God's love for the world is manifested in the incarnation of the Word of God (John 1:1), in the supreme sacrifice on the cross and in the power of the resurrection. It was his mission from the Father, the accomplishment of his will (cf. Luke 22:42; John 5:30). The church, as the body of Christ, is called to this missionary act of self-giving sacrifice and to proclaim the good news of salvation to the world.

In the eucharistic celebration every local church experiences the fullness of the church catholic and prepares itself to address the world through words and deeds of love. The church gathers into one body the whole creation and the joy and the sufferings of all people as it stands in the presence of God in the eucharistic act of praise, thanksgiving and intercession. This inward movement of gathering into one body is accompanied by the outward movement of going forth in mission and service to God's creation. Together, these movements constitute the church's witness to the crucified and risen Christ in whom the unity and the love of the Triune God is manifested in a unique way.

Common witness

In the church's "ecclesial" (*ek-kalô*) movement of calling out, incorporating and building up process, the following major aspects are necessary for its realization today:

1. As Eastern Orthodox and Oriental Orthodox Non-Chalcedonian churches, we need to fully restore the unity in communion of our two families of churches. While we gratefully acknowledge the steps recently taken by our churches towards coming together in mutual love and communion in the one apostolic faith, we wish to emphasize the urgency of the matter for our common witness today. We need to reaffirm our unity in faith above all historic, ethnic, racial, linguistic, national or political loyalties.

2. As active members of the wider ecumenical family of churches, we pray and work for the unity of all in accordance with the will of God expressed in the high-priestly prayer of our Lord. It is our special mission to witness to the apostolic faith of the one undivided church as all churches seek to grow more and more in "one Lord, one faith and one baptism."

3. It is God's *oikoumene* that is the wider context of our unity. Our theological and spiritual heritage is filled with the cosmic dimension of God's salvation. Nothing in the created realm is excluded from this sanctifying and transfiguring power of the Spirit of God. As the liturgical experience shows, the one eucharistic bread stands at the same time for the one church and the totality of creation that we offer to God in thanksgiving. While joyfully celebrating the marvellous gift of creation, we have to commit ourselves to humanity's struggles for human dignity, justice and peace. As Orthodox churches we can witness to the integrity of creation by dedicating ourselves to acts of healing, reconciling, enlightening and saving.

The outgoing ("processional") movement of the church's witness is what we usually call mission. This mission of the church has several points of reference, such as the eternal unity in the Triune God, unity between the divine and human in the incarnate Word of God and the unity between Christ, the head of the church and the church his body. All these dimensions of unity are constitutively qualified by love. The same divine love is the motivating power behind the sending of the Son by the Father and the mission of the comforter Spirit to the church. Thus, the mission of the church is in fact an outreaching processional movement of unity and love.

Therefore, the church, the people of God in the communion of the Holy Spirit, is missionary in its very being, ever proceeding and ever gathering, pulsating with God's all-embracing love and unity. The church, as the presence of the kingdom of God in the world, illuminates in one single reality the glory of God and the eschatological destiny of creation.

The missionary character of the church is expressed in diverse ways and forms: liturgical witness to the transcendent dimension of reality, direct evangelistic witness, witness in secular and pluralistic situations, witness through prayer and asceticism, witnessing the life-giving gospel to the poor and oppressed, witness through committed sharing of the struggle for justice and peace, etc. These are some of the expressions of the outreaching movement of the church's mission.

The constitutive character of mission as the expression of unity calls for a common witness. The situation of our world makes it imperative that what the churches can do together they should not do separately. The search for a common witness helps the churches to come out of their parochial loyalties and encourages them to seek together God's will for our contemporary world.

The Orthodox churches, living in diverse cultures, challenged by their socio-political, economic and linguistic situations, are called upon to engage in a common witness to the one apostolic faith in Christ in new missionary situations. By responding to these challenges creatively and in the unity of the Spirit, without catering to the narrow interests of each individual church, the churches are responding to the will of God.

A serious effort towards creating Orthodox missionary centres and a global missionary strategy will inspire and enable our local Orthodox churches not only to witness along with other Orthodox churches, but also to contribute substantially, from the Orthodox perspective, to other Christian churches engaged in similar forms of witness.

Proselytism

Proselytism, along with the actual disunity among the churches, creates major obstacles for our common witness. Some Christian churches and evangelical bodies are actively engaged in proselytizing Christians already belonging to Orthodox churches. All proselytism by any church should be condemned, and all antagonism and unhealthy competition in mission work should be avoided, as constituting a distorted form of mission.

Unfortunately, well-financed resources and the power of the media in western Europe and America, often play a key role in maintaining the unchristian missionary zeal of those involved in proselytizing efforts. The Orthodox churches have to continue efforts to persuade those churches and agencies involved in proselytism not to engage in dubious missionary activities detrimental to God's will for unity, and to seek the path of true Christian charity and unity.

At the same time, our Orthodox churches have to pay closer attention to the pastoral, educational and spiritual needs of our people and foster in every possible way a continual spiritual renewal in our parishes and monastic communities. It is especially important to develop ways of strengthening family life and caring for the special needs of youth that they might realize the communal love and concern of the church for their well-being and salvation.

The ecumenical vision

One impetus for the modern ecumenical vision was originally inspired by the committed search for a common witness to the good news of salvation. It still remains the primary objective of our ecumenical involvement -- to offer common witness in love to the power of Christ, crucified and risen, so that those who are caught up in this world of division, conflict and death may believe and be transfigured.

III. SOCIAL IMPLICATIONS OF SACRAMENTAL LIFE

The sacramental dimension of life

In the sacrament -- *mysterion* -- of the church, human beings are restored to their proper relationship to God: to communion in Christ with God in the Holy Trinity. Through baptism, chrismation and eucharist, persons receive a new birth in Christ, are anointed in the Spirit and are fully incorporated into the body of Christ -- the church. The gift of this new life in Christ implies a commitment to the renewal of all of life, a conversion of mind and heart, so that God's will may be done, so that the world itself may be transformed and raised up by the witness and work of his children.

In Christ's life, death and resurrection, all creation is restored and sanctified (cf. Eph. 1:10). Our life in Christ, therefore, must become a sacramental life, a life that continues the process of sanctifying all life and all time given to us as God's gift. The church, in the fullness of this sacramental and diaconal life, is and manifests dynamically Christ's presence to the world. Thus, as we participate in the church's life, through fasting, prayer, the celebration of feasts and sacraments, and active service to the poor, we renew ourselves and the entire cosmos, to the extent that our life conforms to Christ in the Holy Spirit.

The struggle to renew all things in God is a daily effort. It involves not merely individuals working for their own salvation, but the corporate work of persons seeking to unite all creation in communion with the living God. Such a life requires humility and sacrifice, self-emptiness, the giving of ourselves to others in love and service, as the Lord gave himself up for us "for the life of the world" (John 6:51). It is life lived in community with others and for others. This is the ecclesial, sacramental reality of life in Christ.

The eucharist and renewal of life

How is this sacramental life developed and nurtured today in the midst of a secular, broken and suffering world? How can all things be united once again in the love and sovereignty of God's kingdom?

For Orthodox Christians, the centre and vivifying force of renewal is the eucharist, where all persons and all creation are gathered together, lifted up, and united in the once-and-for-all offering of Christ himself. The eucharist gives us not only the bread of life necessary for our spiritual sustenance and growth, but lifts up our hearts and minds, enabling us to see with a new vision the life that God has prepared for us from all eternity.

It is in the eucharist that we come to know one another as members of one body, united in the love of Christ in the image of the Holy Trinity. It is in and through this communion in the Spirit that we are given the strength and the power to fulfil Christ's mission in the world.

But this same eucharist is also a judgement for Christians, for we may also partake of it "unto our judgement or condemnation" if this gift of communion is not personally appropriated and realized in our daily lives. We know that through our own weakness and sin, we continue to deny God's love and power in the world. When we ignore the sufferings of our brothers and sisters, when we misuse the gifts of creation through pollution, destruction and waste of natural resources, we create new idols of and for ourselves. Isolated in egocentric self-will and self-indulgence, we cause our own spiritual death and that of our neighbours by indifference, conflict, division and lack of love. We also realize that amidst the joyful unity revealed and given to us within our own church, the awareness of the continuing division of Christians saddens and challenges us.

Prayer and repentance

Consequently, the eucharist and the whole liturgical life of the church calls us to prayer and repentance. Through our common prayer in the church, we learn to pray personally, to offer glory and thanksgiving to God, to pray for ourselves and others, to consider the needs of the whole world, to keep one another alive in Christ through our remembrance of the sick and suffering, those in captivity and persecution, those who have departed this life before us, and especially the martyrs, saints and spiritual fathers and mothers whose witness provides an example for our lives, teaching us the true meaning of the words "Your will be done."

This prayer of Christ to the Father is a continual reminder of the need for repentance and forgiveness of sins. It is a call to re-examine our lives in the light of Christ's life. It is a call addressed personally to each of us for *metanoia* and conversion, a call to literally "turn around" our lives and recommit ourselves to Christ.

Witness and the sacramental life

Finally, for those who have strayed from the communion of the church, as well as for those who have never experienced the newness of her life and joy, the sacraments and the entire life of the church offer opportunities for witness to the truth about God and his relationship to us. Baptisms, marriages, visitations to the sick and dying, ordinations, funerals and rites of blessing, as well as the actual diakonia of the church in social concern and justice, provide unique occasions to proclaim God's message of hope, peace and joy in the crucified and resurrected Lord. It is at these moments, when lives are touched by joy or sorrow, suffering and compassion, that the truths about the ultimate questions of life can awaken minds and hearts to the love of God. It is at these times also that the best witness is the personal witness and presence of the church, through the love and care of her members as a supportive community renewed in faith, love and freedom.

Only in this way, through a sacramental awareness and commitment to the world and a personal offering of ourselves to God, all his children, can we carry on Christ's mission in the world: that all may know "what is the breadth and length and height and depth of the love of Christ...so (that we) may attain to fullness of being, the fullness of God himself" (Eph. 3:18-19).

IV. THE MISSIONARY IMPERATIVE AND RESPONSIBILITY IN THE LOCAL CHURCH

The mission of the local church

The mission of everyone is to know Christ, to live in him and witness to him by word and deed. When our eucharistic assembly experiences this truth, the necessity to share the joy of the resurrection with all people is a natural consequence. This mission includes even those who are baptized, yet ignorant of the calling and election they have received through baptism. It is essential that contemporary means be developed to help them return to the fellowship of the church. The church's mission also calls us to the task of peacemaking, reconciling and defending justice for everyone, especially in contexts where the people of God suffer from injustice, violence, oppression and war. When the eucharistic assembly does not engage in such outreaches it fails to realize its missionary responsibility.

Catholicity of the local church

According to Orthodox ecclesiology, the building up (*oikodome*) of the body of Christ is an essential part of evangelization. Although there are normative forms of local communities, new forms of Christian communities may be necessary due to many social and cultural factors. In the process of building up new communities, the church, through its bishops, must be flexible in their creation.

The mission of the local church suffers when its "catholic" dimension, its ecumenical openness, is not sufficiently underlined and expressed. The local community must not only pray for the *oikoumene*, but must be aware of the necessity to preach the gospel to the whole world. It is the task of each local church to educate missionaries for this work wherever needed.

Some churches have already organized missionary departments to undertake the responsibility of sending missionaries. But the sending of missionaries is an ecclesiological act of establishing a concrete Christian presence in a given nation and culture. The indigenous church must be assisted to develop its own identity and local structure as part of a global fellowship. Every mission outreach should aim to create self-sufficient churches in fellowship with the whole church.

Encouraging various ministries

The church has always recognized the vocation of great missionaries and evangelists. It has also recognized the missionary vocation of the whole people of God, each member of the body of Christ being called in and by the Holy Spirit to mission.

The local bishop has the duty to identify, encourage, help and actualize various forms of lay ministry. The church needs for its evangelistic work catechists, readers, preachers, chanters and all those who participate in the service of the church. In this regard, it is necessary to renew the tradition of the deaconesses. In lay movements and associations, the church possesses an extraordinary missionary network for encouraging the participation of the people of God in mission: men, women, youth, scholars, workers and children.

In addition, monks and nuns may also find a special place in this great task, through prayer and ascetic witness.

Other mission challenges

1. The rise of various extremist Christian sects.

2. The dominating attitude of wealthy and powerful churches towards minority local churches.

3. The resurgence of other religions and various secular ideologies.

4. The disintegration of the family as the basic unit of church and society and problems resulting from broken families and single-parent situtations.

5. The emergence of new cultures, which influence -- positively or negatively -- the spirituality of today's youth.

6. The search for a contemporary code of communication to transmit the message of eternal truth.

RECOMMENDATIONS TO ORTHODOX CHURCHES

The participants in this consultation acknowledge the missionary involvement of their respective churches and the work already done in the mission field. With the following recommendations they aim to encourage the churches to continue, to enlarge and to enrich their missionary efforts all around the world for the sake of a most efficient evangelistic witness today.

1. That the missionary vocation must become a major concern and responsibility in the life of the church and that special programs for mission awareness be organized for men, women and children in various walks of life to help them fulfil their missionary obligation.

2. That Christian education and catechetical material must incorporate the missionary imperative.

3. That theological schools and other educational institutions incorporate missiological studies in their programs, and the training and skills needed for mission.

4. That Orthodox institutes and training centres for mission be established to accept and prepare candidates for work in the mission field. That experienced and qualified Orthodox missionaries be utilized as teachers.

5. That the church institute diaconal ministries, along with liturgical petitions and intercessions with emphasis on mission, for use in local parishes.

6. That special collections in every parish be offered for mission and that a special place be established for mission information and promotion.

7. That Associations or Friends of Missionaries be organized for moral and material support of those engaged in mission.

8. That regional forums be established for coordination, cooperation and sharing of the Orthodox mission resources of the various churches.

9. That Orthodox publications -- especially translations -- be utilized for the support of mission work.

10. That the church renew the vocations of the deaconesses, catechists, readers, musicians and preachers for particular service in the mission field.

11. That the churches call monks and nuns to establish a monastic witness, in places where missions are being established, as spiritual centers.

12. That all churches set aside a special time each year for the promotion and support of missions.

13. That Orthodox churches join with other Christian churches in increasing their moral and financial support for the work of the World Council of Churches in general and the Commission on World Mission and Evangelism (CWME) in particular.

RECOMMENDATIONS TO THE ECUMENICAL COMMUNITY

1. That the Commission on World Mission and Evangelism of the World Council of Churches encourage and support young people in the study of missiology.

2. That all churches review and reflect upon their missionary programs in the light of their impact on the faithful of other churches to avoid mistakes or grievances that have occurred in the past and to prevent antagonism and competition in future mission work.

3. That through the CWME and related organizations educational programs be promoted to better inform members of all churches about the role of historic and present mission work of the Orthodox churches.

4. That prior to, during and after the World Conference in San Antonio, Texas, 22 May - 1 June 1989, delegates be encouraged to become informed about Orthodox mission activity in North America and elsewhere through study and visits.

ORTHODOX MISSION

PAST, PRESENT, FUTURE

ORTHODOX MISSION

PAST, PRESENT, FUTURE

Bishop ANASTASIOS of Androussa

Orthodox witness is imbued with the desire to carry out God's will in a loving and heroic manner. The "living in Christ" and the "following in his footsteps" has always been the ideal, the heart of Orthodox spirituality. The central longing of Orthodox worship is expressly stated in the supplication of the liturgy of the Presanctified Gifts, when the faithful pray to the Father: "That partaking ... of these divine gifts, and receiving new life through them, we may be united unto thy Christ himself, ...; that with thy Word, O Lord, dwelling in us, and walking in us we may become the temple of thy Holy and ever venerated Spirit...". The transforming glory and power of the Trinitarian God must shine forth in time, in every manifestation of human life, and throughout the creation, through the mission of the church.

Since the key word "mission" -- around which our discussions will revolve -- is often used with different nuances, it is necessary to state that by this word we mean witness to the living Trinitarian God, who calls all to salvation and binds human beings together in the church, who otherwise would not belong to it or who have lost their tie to it. This characteristic distinguishes it from mere pastoral care, which is directed towards those already incorporated in the church. The field of Christian mission today is both the distant geographical regions of the third world (more precisely, of the world of two-thirds of the total population), and the rest of the inhabited world. It is henceforth a question of mission to all six continents. For every local church, mission is "inward" or "internal," when it takes place within its geographical, linguistic and cultural bounds, and "outward" or "external" when it reaches beyond these bounds to other nations and lands.

The church, "the one, holy, catholic and apostolic church," is obliged to witness to those near and afar, and to show interest in the whole human being, both on a personal and a social level, for the progress of the whole world. Nothing relating to human existence is out of the scope of interest for Orthodox mission.

I. A QUICK GLANCE AT THE PAST: BASIC PRINCIPLES OF BYZANTINE AND RUSSIAN MISSIONS

When, more than thirty years ago, there was a revival in contemporary Orthodoxy of the ideal of an external mission -- especially following the "Porefthentes" movement, which sprang from the Fourth General Assembly of "Syndesmos" here in Thessaloniki (1958) -- we had to face two difficulties: the amazement of westerners, who thought the Orthodox church was introspective and uninterested in mission; and a pathetic internal opposition from Orthodox, who considered such an interest as something imported. For this reason, during the first decade, not only was external mission stressed as an Orthodox theological and ecclesiological necessity, but a special attempt was made to study its history.

From the relevant documents published during these last decades, it has become ever clearer that the "apostolic" duty is a basic element of being Orthodox[1], even if, under certain historical circumstances, the evangelical activity of certain local churches has slowed down and interest in mission has become lethargic.

This year's anniversary of the millenium of the Baptism of Rus' sheds further light both on the missionary initiatives of the

Byzantines and on the apostolic activities of their Russian disciples in later centuries.

a) Throughout the millenium of its existence, Orthodox Byzantium concerned itself with the broadcasting of the Christian faith, either to the heathen within its boundaries, or to the pagan tribes pouring into the Empire, as well as to neighbouring countries. More particularly, we can distinguish two periods of intense missionary zeal: a) from the fourth to the sixth century, culminating at the time of Justinian, and b) during the ninth and eleventh centuries, under the Macedonian Dynasty. In the first and second periods, apostolic activity was combined with a deeper theological search and a spiritual blossoming.

During the first period, the missionary task fell to enlightened bishops, such as St John Chrysostom (+ 407), and to holy monks, such as the Saints Hilarion (+ 371), Euthymios (+ 473) and Sabbas (+ 532). The Byzantines took an interest in the evangelization of peoples bordering on the Empire, such as the Goths, the Huns, the Iberians and certain tribes of Colchis and the Caucasus. Following the Christianization of the Ethiopians, they even took an interest in the evangelization of Nubian tribes to the south, and to the northern reaches of what is today Tunisia. Because this missionary activity took place in areas where there was later to be a great mingling of populations, little is known about this first period.

The second period, linked to the conversion of the Slavs, has been better investigated; especially during the last few years, worldwide interest has focused on the 1100th anniversary of the missions of the Saints Cyril and Methodius, as well as on the afore-mentioned millenium.

The Byzantine mission was based on certain clear-cut and essential principles. At the forefront was a desire to create an authentic local eucharistic community. Thus precedence was given to translating the Holy Scriptures, the liturgical texts and the writings of the Fathers, as well as to the building of beautiful churches which would proclaim -- with the eloquent silence of beauty -- that God had come to live amongst humanity. The importance attached by Byzantine theology to a life of worship and "divinization" did not prevent direct interest in the social and cultural dimensions of life. Together with the gospel, the Byzantines transfused into their converted peoples the whole of their experience -- political, artistic, economic, cultural -- permeated by evangelical principles and the Christian vision of life. They contributed to the self-awareness developed by the young nations, along with their own culture.

Together with the power of the gospel, which it infused into the waves of uncultured peoples overunning Europe, Christian Byzantium brought them a completely new life: spiritual, social and political.

The flexibility and understanding with which the Greek missionaries adapted the Byzantine liturgy and tradition to local circumstances gave them an ecumenical character and caused them to serve as a bond among the various Orthodox peoples. At the same time, the development of the vernacular and of a national temperament among these peoples -- for which many Byzantine missionaries toiled with such reverence and tenderness -- helped preserve the personality of the converted peoples. Far from indulging in an administrative centralization and a monolithic conception of the church, the Byzantine missionaries saw the unity of the extended church in its joint thanksgiving, with many voices but in one spirit, and in the sacramental participation of all in the cup of life, "For as there is but one bread, so we who are many, are but one body." Finally, missionary work in Byzantium was not carried out by a handful of "specialists." Bishops, priests, monks, emperors -- whether of great or of medium stature -- princesses, diplomats, officers, soldiers, merchants, mariners, emigrants, travellers, captives[2], were all involved. The modest and patient heroism shown in this direction by thousands of known and unknown Byzantines during the centuries-long life of the Empire, forces the student of history to agree with what

Charles Diehl wrote concerning the conversion of the Slavs: "Missionary work was one of the glories of Byzantium."[3]

b) The Russian missionary epic is also fascinating and extraordinarily rich: during the first period, which extends from the baptism of the inhabitants of Kiev to the Mongol conquest (988-1240), monasteries and convents sprang up, and there was a great missionary impulse as enlightened bishops, priests, and monks worked heroically for the evangelization of the Slavic tribes to the north. In the second period, from the Mongol invasion to roughly the end of the fifteenth century, a great number of monks retired to the forests and built hermitages that became centres of missionary and cultural activity. Prisoners of war became the first "apostles" of the Tartars. Apart from the anonymous bearers of the gospel, this period is famous for its great missionary personalities, such as Stephen of Perm (+ 1396). During the third period, from the sixteenth to the eighteenth century, hundreds of thousands of Muslims from the local population around Kazan entered the church. As the Empire extended into Siberia, where Christianity was, until then, unknown, churches and monasteries mushroomed, yet their number was insufficient to cover the local needs. At that time, state policy was often hostile to mission. Nevertheless, great missionary figures, such as St Trifon of Novgorod (+ 1583), who brought the gospel to the Lapps, Bishop Filotei of Tobolsk (+ 1727) and others, through their missionary zeal, drew thousands to Christ. The fourth period, lasting from the nineteenth century to the Russian Revolution (1917), bears a more ecclesial stamp and is most fruitful. The missionaries are numerous: bishops, priests, monks, laypersons -- people like the monk Makary Glukharev (+ 1847), apostle of the warlike tribes of the forbidding Altai mountain range; Bishop Innokentiy Veniaminov (later Metropolitan of Moscow), who worked among the Aleutians, the Eskimos and other Alaskan tribes; St Herman, also in Alaska; the merchant Sidenikoff among the Samoyeds; the philologist and theologian Ilminsky, who introduced new methods of translation and missionary work among the Tartars. Many were the tribes towards which the Russian missionary effort was directed; many were the languages into which the gospel was translated.

In all this, a great contribution was made by the Orthodox Missionary Society, which was founded in Moscow in 1870 and which undertook to give financial support to the Russian missionaries. Another great contribution was made by the Kazan Academy, which became a centre of missionary studies; its department of translations published books in dozens of languages belonging to such regions as the Volga, Siberia, the Caucasus, etc.

Russian missionaries were active, too, outside the Empire, in China, Korea and Japan; their number included such champions of mission as Bishop Innokentiy Figurovsky in China and Archbishop Nikola Kasatkin (1836-1912) in Japan.[4]

The Russian missionaries were inspired by the principles of Byzantine Orthodoxy and developed them with originality and daring: the creation of an alphabet for unwritten languages; the translation of biblical and liturgical texts into new tongues; the celebration of the liturgy in local dialects, with systematic philological care; the preparation of a native clergy as quickly as possible; the joint participation of clergy and laity, with an emphasis on the mobilization of the faithful; care for the educational, agricultural, and artistic or technical development of the tribes and peoples drawn to Orthodoxy. Continuing the Orthodox tradition, they gave importance to liturgical life, to the harmonious architecture of the churches, to the beauty of worship and to its social consequences. Certain fundamental principles, only now being put into use by western missions, were always the undoubted base of the Orthodox missionary efforts.

c) Many Orthodox churches, forced to live under Islamic regimes -- four centuries of Turkish occupation in the Balkans and thirteen centuries of Arab domination in Egypt -- were, of course, not in a position to organize missions abroad. On the contrary: in order to ward off the terrible danger of the conversion of the Christian population to Islam, they were obliged to fight hard to keep control of their flock and to win back, from time to time, those who had strayed. This lengthy effort, which amounted to an heroic resistance to varied and powerful non-Christian pressures, added thousands of new martyrs to the church.[5]

Even in the twentieth century, in countries where fanatical anti-religious regimes have taken power, the Orthodox church has lived its missionary task in the form of *resistance* -- firmly, calmly, in accordance with the ethos of the early Christians. It has provided some of the most heroic and authentic chapters of church history, which await a systematic study.

d) We should look, however, at another aspect of the past. When we Orthodox find ourselves in a western setting, we automatically tend to describe our church in glowing colours. We often have also a tendency to compare our own achievements with the shortcomings of others. It is now time, when analyzing the past, to become more objective. This is, moreover, imposed by the Orthodox ethos, which is guided by the light of the Holy Spirit. Studying historical facts in such an "Orthodox" spirit, we need to pay attention not only to the highwater marks of Orthodox mission, but also to periods of bleakness and lethargy. The former led to new creations, such as the baptizing of numerous peoples, and especially the Slavs. The hours of lethargy and omission provoked historical evolutions and socio-religous upheavals that were unbelievably costly for Orthodoxy. The lack of interest in Byzantium for a proper consequential and perpetual outward mission contributed to the evolution of a spiritual vacuum that encouraged Islam in the Arabian world, and finally helped to bring down the Byzantine Empire. If, in the fourth, fifth and sixth centuries, the Byzantine church had made a proper translation of the scriptures into Arabic, to foster a cultural identity among the Arabs, as it did later -- in the ninth and tenth centuries -- for the Slavs and the Russians of the north, developments in the south, and its own fate, would have been quite different.

Later on, too, the lukewarm "internal mission" of the Russian steppe, the lack of sensitivity to social developments and to the application of Christian ideals in the social and political spheres, contributed to the development of Marxism-Leninism, which has taken hold of most of the Orthodox countries in our century. Both of these utterly divergent socio-political realities -- Islam and Leninism -- sprang from geographical, and also frequently cultural, areas in which Orthodoxy had developed and which allowed them to blossom out, each eclectically absorbing diverse elements of it. One could even be so bold as to see in these two systems radical "heresies" of the Orthodox East. Islam adopted fragments of Orthodox Christianity, twisting them into odd shapes, while Lenin's socialist ideology transformed other characteristics of the Russian Orthodox mentality, such as the heroic ideal of the spiritual struggle and the eschatological vision of a brotherhood of humankind.

II. CONTEMPORARY PERIOD: DEVELOPMENT OF NEW ORTHODOX CHURCHES

Socio-political conditions, such as have developed in many local Orthodox churches, and the danger of deviation on the part of the people, have, in our time, brought about a particular emphasis on "internal mission" (that which is carried out within the geographical, linguistic and political confines of the local church). We can distinguish three separate settings in which the local Orthodox churches have been obliged to live and give their witness today: a) the Muslim setting, in which move chiefly the bishoprics belonging to the ancient Orthodox Patriarchates; b) the socialist-Marxist setting, in which many churches continue to develop in eastern Europe; c) the new, secularized, pluralistic and technocratic setting, with its swollen agnostic current, in which the Orthodox churches of the "diaspora" find themselves in western Europe, America and recently in Greece.

All these settings exercise a wide variety of pressures, often with pulverizing results, on certain local churches. Other speakers at our consultation have taken it upon themselves to present the particular circumstances and problems of the local, traditional Orthodox churches. Here I shall restrict myself to mentioning some facts relative to the new churches formed in our day and age, in Africa and Asia, and the centres responsible for supporting external missions[6]. The missionary Orthodox churches of Africa and Asia, though numerically small, have opened up an important chapter in the history of Orthodoxy. They are contributing to the transplantation of Orthodoxy into new regions, although their number is not impressive. Compared to other churches, the results are poor. But in comparison with the past, they show serious growth, and are a hopeful "nursery" for the future.

a) We shall start with the mission being carried out under the immediate ecclesiastical jurisdiction of the Ecumenical Patriarchate of Constantinople. The Orthodox church in Korea today has four church buildings and parishes in relatively big cities, two Korean priests and about 2,000 members. They are supported by two missionary priests, two laymen and three nuns, all from Greece. To prepare native staff, a seminary functions three afternoons a week. In recent years, many Orthodox books have been translated into the Korean language, both liturgical and of a more general, historical or edifying nature. Orthodox groups have also been developed in Hong Kong and Singapore. In India recently two Orthodox parishes in Arabah, 100 km from Calcutta, have been created. Two Indian priests have been ordained, and a missionary is working there.

b) More extended is the missionary effort undertaken under the jurisdiction of the Patriarchate of Alexandria and All Africa. The first Orthodox groups have been formed in East Africa through the initiative of the Africans themselves. Today there are roughly 210 Orthodox parishes and small communities there, served by 75 African clergy and 50 reader-catechists. The main body of Orthodox is to be found in

Kenya, where there are 85 parishes and 67 smaller communities. They run 10 nursery schools, 5 primary schools, 1 secondary school and 3 dispensaries. The number of faithful exceeds 60,000. The missionary team consists of the bishop, a priest, 2 nuns and 8 lay people, sent and financed by the churches of Greece, Finland, America and Cyprus. This inter-Orthodox collaboration is a new trait in the history of Orthodox mission.

The Orthodox church in Uganda has 29 parishes, served by an African auxiliary bishop and 14 African priests. The number of faithful is roughly estimated to be 10,000. Quite a number of Ugandans have studied abroad. The mission runs 2 secondary schools, 10 primary schools and a polyclinic managed by a doctor who has studied in Athens. There are also 4 dispensaries. The country has suffered from civil war, and many plans for rebuilding churches and other centres are behind time.

The Orthodox church in Tanzania, which has taken shape in the last 8 years, has 9 parishes, 21 small communities and 9 church buildings. The number of faithful is put at 8,000. Recently 3 dispensaries were built and equipped. The African clergy totals 4 priests and 2 deacons.

In Nairobi, the "Orthodox Patriarchal Seminary Makarios III, Archbishop of Cyprus" has been functioning since 1982. At present it has 12 teachers and 47 students.

The Orthodox of East Africa belong to different tribes. To meet liturgical needs, the divine liturgy of St John Chrysostom has been published in Swahili, Kikuyu, Luya and Luganda; other liturgical translations have also been made into these languages, as well as into Haya and Lufo, and translations with a view to publication are being made into Nandi and Lango.

In Central Africa, two big missionary centres have been established, one in Kanaga and the other in Koluwezi, Zaire. There are 49 parishes and roughly 9,000 Orthodox in the country, served by 22 Zairois clergy. The local church is assisted by two Greek archimandrites and 12 lay people. There are also secondary school, a primary school, a small seminary for future priests, a hostel for young people and a foreign medical service. For purposes of worship and catechism, French, Swahili and local dialects are used.

In West Africa there exist: in Cameroon, one Orthodox community with 2 native priests; in Ghana (since 1977), 12 Orthodox parishes, with 9 church buildings served by 5 native priests and 2 deacons. The divine liturgy, a summary of church history, and the services of baptism, marriage and burial have all been translated into Fanti. In Nigeria there are 16 parishes served by 1 missionary priest and 9 native priests, with 12 church buildings, 4 primary schools and a number of nursery schools.

The spectrum of missionary work is wide. And it grows ever wider, for example, when we meditate on the responsibility that every local church has for helping the people in matters of sanitation, education and culture[6]. All the expressions of human life need to be transformed through the grace of the Trinitarian God.

The prayer and vision of all of us is to see the establishment of true local African churches, capable of assuming by themselves the preaching of the gospel, self-governing and self-supporting. But in order to consolidate these churches, there needs to be given, during the coming decades, serious and continuous assistance from the older Orthodox churches, coupled with theological and pastoral guidance.

c) The Churches of Alaska, Japan and China are special cases. The first one is now within the USA, and is mainly concerned with mission as an internal affair, consolidating the population there (Aleutians, Eskimos and others) in the Orthodox faith resisting the technological current of American society, which is undermining their racial tradition and, with it, their Orthodoxy. The church there is served by 26 native priests under a Russian bishop. The training of native clergy is carried out by St Herman Seminary, which has been functioning on Kodiak Island since 1972 and has close ties with St Vladimir's Seminary.

The Church of Japan is already a hundred years old. The leadership and all the activities are in Japanese hands. Like a tiny islet amid the archipelago of Japanese society -- so dynamic, hastening so dizzily towards the new era of electronics -- it has also to face the great technological provocation upsetting the western world. At the moment, the Japanese Orthodox Church has in its bosom some 30,000 Japanese Orthodox, who attend to the upkeep of 150 church buildings and are served by an archbishop-metropolitan and 35 Japanese priests. It is certain that cooperation with the older, bigger Orthodox churches will contribute to its development. The type of spiritual assistance required will be decided on by itself.

The case of the Church of China is more complicated. All that is left of the endeavours of the Russian Orthodox missionaries is a flickering candle-flame. Most of the Orthodox church buildings have been pulled down (Peking, Tien-Tsin, Harbin). In 1983 a church building was inaugurated in Harbin, and it is now served by a Chinese Orthodox priest. Recently there have been rumours of another Orthodox community in Urumchi. The most immediate problem is the preparation and ordination of new Chinese Orthodox clergymen to look after the "small remnant" of Orthodox in this vast country, allowing that the installing of foreign missionaries is strictly forbidden. It may be that the new candle of Orthodoxy lit in Hong Kong, will prove valuable for preserving the flame of Orthodoxy in China.

d) In many local Orthodox churches, alongside a growing interest in biblical studies, patristic texts and liturgy, we are still living a simple flowering: first, a longing for monasticism, with, at its peak, the renewal taking place on Mount Athos and, second, a revival of missionary zeal. Its first goal has been "internal mission," and during the last few years it has been complemented by the return of "external mission." The resurgence of the monastic ideal, with its insistance on personal *metanoia* as a way of life, expresses the need for a closer adherence to the spirit of the gospel; it is doubtless contributing to the coming of God's kingdom and the carrying out of his will both in personal living and in the world at large. The missionary revival, with its accent on the apostolicity and catholicity of the church, is a reminder that the gift of *metanoia* and salvation should by no means be turned into a private, individual affair. Our duty is to live a life centred on the church, making its horizons our own -- and these horizons extend worldwide, "ecumenically." It is a gift destined for the whole world, to everybody, given so as to transform all things. Christ was crucified for the sake of the whole world. And those who are crucified with him, are crucified for the sake of all. They are set apart from the world, but their prayer, attuned to the prayer of Christ, embraces the suffering and the hopes of all humanity and all creation. "Blessed is the monk who is separated from all and in harmony with all," maintain the first books of the Philokalia.[7]

I believe that from those two currents, and especially from the combination of the monastic rebirth and the revival of the Orthodox missionary awareness, fruits will ripen to maturity and be of benefit to contemporary Orthodoxy. The whole world is secretly longing for an authentic presentation of the gospel of truth, of freedom, of love and of the new life in Christ. It is yearning for holiness.

More particularly, during the past thirty years, great strides have been made in the development and support of external mission. Centres and groups have been created with this as their sole aim. The oldest of these associations, *Porefthentes*, is an offshoot of the Orthodox youth movement *Syndesmos* -- as we have already stated. It blossomed out at the beginning of 1959 with the publication in Greek and English of a magazine of the same name, which continued to appear for ten years. For its irreproachable collecting and managing of funds, it received legal recognition in Greece (1961), but never lost its inter-Orthodox approach to matters. Later its example was followed, on a local level, by *Hoi Philoi tes Ougandas* (The Friends of Uganda) in Thessaloniki (1963), which later on took the name *Hellenike Adelphotes Orthodoxou Exôterikes Hierapostoles* (Greek Brotherhood of Orthodox External Mission), and by *Ho Prôtokletos* (The First-Called) in Patras (1974). Recently smaller groups have been formed in various Greek towns.

From its inception, *Porefthentes* declared that it was not aiming at founding a separate movement, but was putting all its efforts, projects, programmes, research, publications and personnel at the church's disposal, for the creation of a wider ecclesiastical missionary activity. So, with members of the *Porefthentes* staff as pioneers, the *Grapheion Exôterikes Hierapostoles* (Bureau of External Mission) was founded in 1968 within the framework of the *Apostoliki Diakonia* of the Church of Greece, and a Week of External Mission was adopted by all the Metropolias of Greece. In 1969 its director was invited to assist in the creation of the Desk for "Research and Relations with Orthodox" at the World Council of Churches. In 1971, the *Kentron Hierapostolikôn Spoudôn* (Centre for Missionary Studies) was organized, with the collaboration of the Holy Synod and the Theological Faculty of the University of Athens, and functioned up to 1976. In 1972, the first ladies' monastic group was set up, which later developed into the Convent of St John the Precursor, Kareas, with the aim of serving and supporting missionary work; in 1976, at Athens University, there was created a Chair of Missiology. Since 1981 *Porefthentes* has taken on the editing of the official missionary magazine of the Church of Greece, *Panta ta Ethne* (All Nations).

At the beginning of the 1960s, efforts were made to extend the organization of *Porefthentes* to other Orthodox churches too, and similar groups of "*Syndesmos*" were created in Finland, America and other countries where there were Orthodox youth movements. However, the well-known autonomy of the ecclesiastical jurisdictions did not favour this effort at coordination and, finally, in each local church there developed other structures, in accordance with local conditions. In Finland, a "Mission Office of the Finnish Orthodox Church" (Ortodoksinen Lähetysry) has come into existence (1981), while in the Americas there exists the "Mission Center of the Greek Orthodox Archdiocese of North and South America"; the latter was organized on a permanent basis in 1985, systematically extending the work of the old "Commission for Mission," which had begun in 1963.

In the realm of theoretical investigation into mission in the Orthodox tradition, a significant contribution has been made by the "Desk for Research and Relations with Orthodox," named later on "Desk for Orthodox Studies and Relationships" of the World Council of Churches, which has organized a series of consultations on specific themes[8]. Thus an opportunity has been given both to Orthodox circles making a systematic study of mission, and to ecumenical missionary bodies, with a view to enriching their experience through contact with Orthodox concepts.

e) In spite of the facts mentioned so far, we have to admit that the missionary work of the Orthodox Church on new frontiers in non-Christian regions remains very limited. Of course, we have never stopped confessing our faith in the "one, holy, catholic and apostolic Church." Yet, it would not be an exaggeration to say that, in many cases, Orthodox identification with the catholic and apostolic aspects of the church is expressed rather weakly. The fault lies, to some extent, with the excessive nationalism of the local churches. Certainly, every nation that has become Orthodox owes a lot to Orthodoxy, which has strengthened not only its sense of personal dignity, but also a sense of the value of its nationhood. But this national gratitude and self-consciousness has often led to a turning inward, to a dangerous deviation theologically, and to a nationalistic, psychological imperviousness. There is thus a syndrome that often inhibits Orthodox mission: the idea that our own responsibility is restricted to our own area, and that the problems of others are "none of our business." But on this planet, no people and no social unit can live in isolation. There is a reciprocal influence. And in our times, interdependence is growing rapidly.

The lack of continuity in Orthodox missionary endeavour has been and remains another of our basic weaknesses. Frequently the call to mission appears as the sudden spiritual exaltation of an era, as an exception, which does not leave in its wake structures and institutions on an inter-Orthodox basis, to ensure an Orthodox presence on difficult fronts. It is time we asked ourselves why the Orthodox mission to China, after centuries of hard struggle, has had such poor results. As the snows of persecution are melting in China in our days, and while, like ears of corn, hundreds of Protestant and Roman Catholic communities are sprouting again, the Orthodox are only two. Was the Orthodox mission perhaps tainted with too much nationalism? Why, in these twentieth century trials, were not other Orthodox moved to carry on the relay and rush in to help? That happened, for example, when the German Lutherans in East Africa turned over the responsibility for continuing their mission to the Scandinavians. Also: why, while the Orthodox mission began almost simultaneously with the Protestant in Korea, do the Protestants in that country today number five and one-half million and the Orthodox a bare 2,000? Still other painful questions need to be asked when we review sixty years of Orthodox Church presence in Uganda. Can its development be considered satisfactory in comparison with the progress of the other churches? We should stop generalizing, simplifying and embellishing the facts. Clearheadedness is needed, and a unbiased study of the past. Not, of course, in order to judge or to condemn others. But to set out aright on the path to the future, with a sense of responsibility, with sufficient seriousness of purpose, and in accordance with our possibilities.

Finally, there is the danger of thinking that the missionary task is fulfilled when the faithful indulge in mutual support. Mission, however, is not accomplished by just attending to "our own folk." It is not synonymous with pastoral care[9], though it is closely linked to it. It is not right to call every spiritual effort "mission," and to reassure ourselves that our missionary duty ends with church activities. Mission is principally the binding of "nonbelievers" to the church; those who have become indifferent or hostile to the faith; those who refuse, in theory or in practice, the teaching and principles of that faith. The type of sensitivity needed is one that leads the bishops, priests and frequent church-goers to another attitude towards those outside the faith. Not an attitude of antipathy or of crossing swords with them, but an effort to understand their language, problems, reservations, temptations, questionings, sinfulness, even their enmity. It leads, finally, to an attempt to overcome existing barriers through the strength of truth, prayer and love.

III. TOWARDS THE DEVELOPMENT OF ORTHODOX MISSION

For the growth of Orthodox mission in the future, two things are of fundamental importance. First, the development of missionary thought and awareness by all members of the church that mission is not a supplement or an appendix, but rather a basic expression of our ecclesiastical self-understanding and self-conscience, and it is necessary that this be transferred to our ecclesiastical structures.

Second, a sober study of the modern world, the new, electronic, universal civilization that emerges from the setting of the second millenium and the understanding of its pluralistic character.

1. The theological understanding of mission is not a necessity for the theologians only. It is of decisive importance for the whole church. For this reason, we must briefly underline some fundamental theological truths.[10]

a) A firm basis of every missionary effort is taking into consideration and moving in the light of the Revelation and especially of *the mystery of the Trinity*. The starting point of any apostolic activity on our behalf, is the promise and order of the Risen Lord in its Trinitarian perspective: "As the Father has sent me, even so I send you ... Receive the Holy Spirit" (John 20:21-22). The love of the Father has been expressed through the *sending* of the Son. "For God so loved the world that he gave his only Son....For God sent the Son into the world" (John 3:16-17).

The Son then sends his disciples, with the power of the Holy Spirit, to call all the children of God, who were dispersed, in his kingdom. All, men and women, created in the likeness of God, must return to the freedom of love, share in the life of love of the three persons of the Holy Trinity. God's glory, which radiates upon all creatures, has to transform all things, and "to be raised upon the earth and upon the heavens."

The sending of the Son forms the beginning, and defines more especially Christian mission. The work of the Son is not simply an announcement, it is an event. The Incarnation, which is the "assuming" of human nature, is the most predominant event in the history of the universe, the recreation for its regeneration within the life of the Holy Trinity. It opens the way for the *eschaton*, the fulfilment of the world's evolution.

This "assuming" in love, the continuous transfer of life in love, the transfiguration of all things in the light of God's glory is being continued in space and time through the mission of the church, the body of Christ.

The conjunction "as," which is found in John 20:21, remains very decisive for Orthodox mission. It is I who always remains your model, Christ stresses. You must walk in my footsteps and follow my example. Christological dogma defines the way of the mission of the Trinitarian God, which the faithful continue. The most crucial point in mission is not what one announces, but what one lives, what one *is*. Humankind is "becoming" as much as they remain in Christ. "Being in Christ" forms the heart of mission. "He who abides in me, and

I in him, he it is that bears much fruit, for apart from me you can do nothing" (John 15:5).

From the very beginning, the Holy Spirit shares in the sending of the Son. The Incarnation is realized "by the Holy Spirit and the Virgin Mary." The Spirit cooperates with the one who is the best of humankind: the all Holy Virgin Mary, who without reservation and with much joy submits herself to the will of God, for the realization of the mission of the Son. It is the Spirit in the form of a dove, who at the Jordan river seals the beginning of the public ministry of the Son. In the form of tongues of fire and "like the rush of a mighty wind," the Spirit creates the church, transforming the scared disciples into brave apostles, full of divine light, knowledge and power. It is the Spirit that unceasingly gives life to the church and all members within, transforming them into a living temple of the mystical body of Christ, enabling them to share in the safeguarding of Christ's mission for the salvation of the whole world. The energies of the Trinitarian God are always personal, "from the Father through the Son in the Spirit." This trinitarian faith is to be found in the depth of our thoughts and actions.

b) The strengthening of the Orthodox missionary conscience brings about a deeper understanding of Orthodox *ecclesiology*, and vice versa. In the era of the New Testament, when so many terms had defined the different religious communities, groups and societies, the first faithful, in order to define and express their self-awareness, chose the word *"ecclêsia,"* a word that means the gathering of the people of the whole city. In this new reality, in the new eschatological "city," which was erected upon the cross and the empty tomb of the resurrected Lord, God is calling upon us, the city, which is the whole oecumene, the inhabited earth. During the reigns of the various empires and kingdoms, the new community gathered by the Triune God, choosing the term *"ecclêsia"* as a name of identity, wanted also, through it, to underline the responsible participation of all its members.

We cannot forget that we belong to the "catholic" church, which embraces all things (*"ta panta"*), the whole of humanity.

We Orthodox often stress the tradition of the ancient church, according to which, when speaking about the Catholic Church of a concrete city, is meant the "church" which is present in its fullness in each eucharistic local gathering. As the whole Christ is present in the sacrament of the holy eucharist, in the same way the church, his mystical body, keeps its fullness in the local "catholic" church.

Nevertheless, this basic thesis does not abolish the other great truth that, from the beginning, the apostles' perspective and aim had been to spread the gospel "to the end of the earth," to invite all nations to enter the Church. "Go ye and make disciples of all nations" (Matt. 28:19). No person is excepted. No local church has the right to individually enjoy the Christian gospel and keep it exclusively as its own treasure. The basic duty of every local "catholic" church remains therefore to live the whole tradition and offer it *"catholicôs,"* in its fullness; in peace, but decisively, in a universal perspective. The word "Orthodox" was first used as an adjective: "Orthodox Catholic Church," that is, a truly "catholic" church -- having a true faith and a true worship -- with the two meanings previously mentioned. The understanding of these two sides of the "catholicity" of our church must be stressed more and more.

Furthermore, it is time for us to experience this "apostolicity" in a more consequent way, not only placing emphasis on the "apostolicity" of the tradition and the apostolic succession, but also by living the apostolic dynamic and self-conscience of the church and strengthening the apostolic mind and apostolic responsibility of all the faithful. When we confess our belief in the "one, holy, catholic and apostolic church," we simultaneously declare our duty to share in her "apostolic" mission.

The centre of Orthodox spiritual and missionary life is the holy eucharist by which we become "one body with Christ." Thus, by sharing in his life, we share in his mission. The "being" in Christ is not expressed through a mystical or emotional escape, but rather in continuous following his steps. "He who says he abides in him ought to walk in the same way in which he walked" (I John 2:6).

c) By participating in mission we share in a divine plan, which is still in evolution and has *cosmic dimensions.* We are already moving within the *eschatological era.*

Through the outpouring of the Holy Spirit and the formation of the church, and through the continuous presence of the Spirit, a process of transfiguration of human life has begun, which raises humanity and transforms the universe. Mission is a presupposition of the coming of the kingdom. "And this gospel of the kingdom will be preached throughout the whole world, as a testimony to all nations; and then the end will come" (Matt. 24:14).

Within the eschatological era all things have universal dimensions. A basic element of this is surprise, the breaking down of things conventionally accepted. Neither "those who have done good" nor "those who have done evil" had ever thought that the basis of the Last Judgement would be how much they had been able to recognize Christ in the humble and poor of the earth with whom he identifies himself. "...As you did it not to one of the least of these..." (Matt. 25:45). Our participation in the suffering of people who are in need is essentially meeting the Lord who suffered for us. This view makes Christian eschatology ever and ever revolutionary, missionary and opportune at the same time.

According to Orthodox thought, the world is led to a transformation. The whole universe has been invited to enter the church, to become the church of Christ, in order to become after the end of centuries the heavenly kingdom of

God. "The Church is the centre of the universe, the sphere in which its destinies are determined".[11]

The thought that has been developed mainly by the Greek Fathers, that the human person must comprise the whole world in his/her ascent towards the personal God, designates the Orthodox respect not only to every human person, but also to nature. All things (*ta panta*) will find their own *logos* (reason), which is Christ. "All things in heaven and things on earth." It is in this "mystery of the will of God" (Eph. I:9-10) that we participate when we work for mission. This perspective frees us from any individualistic piety, any tendency to marginalize the apostolic effort.

2. In the Gospel of St Mark, mission is connected more intensively with "the whole world" and "the whole creation." "Go into all the world and preach the gospel to the whole creation" (Mark 16:15). We Christians must take this *world* and *creation* into serious consideration and study it continuously, in its evolution, multiformity, pluralism and dynamism.

a) Absorbed many times by the marked historical conscience that characterizes our church, many Orthodox have very often oriented themselves towards the past. Nevertheless, the eschatological dimension, which we have already spoken about, remains a basic aspect of the Orthodox theological inheritence. The head of the Church is he "who is, who was, and who is to come, the Almighty" (Rev. 1:8). Consequently, the future should be for us another basic field of vision.

In this scope, the serious theological study of the new emerging civilization and new means of communication, which combines together the whole of humankind and contributes to the interdependence and inter-penetration of thoughts, insights and customs, is necessary. It is incumbent on us to face seriously the tremendous revolution which is pushing humanity from the old industrial era to a universal electronic culture, to a world society of interdependence. The old passage from the *oral word* to the written one, formely offered tremendous possibilities to humankind for storing knowledge and experience, and decisively accelerated human progress and evolution. The new passage from the written word to the "electronic word" has opened infinite possibilities for accumulating universal knowledge and created a new human intelligence. The gospel must also play a crucial role in the forthcoming new culture.

Closely related to this is the new type of life experienced in big cities. Today, city dwellers comprise about one half of the world's population and there are about 3,050 cities having a population of more than 100,000, and about 296 "megacities," each with over one million in population.[12]

But parallel to the search for the ways to spread the gospel of hope within these new situations and new languages is the need for an understanding of the new existential problems that are created by modern atheism, agnosticism, secularism: the being absorbed by everyday earthly activity, which pushes every spiritual interest into the shadow of indifference. The responsible and serious dialogue in modern currents of thought, which allows the accomplishments of science, is a fundamental task for us.

In many instances, the leadership of the Orthodox Church has been limited to a marginal, "worshipping only" role and has been indifferent to approaching the intellectuals and artists, who easily catch the vibrations of modern problems and then send them forth, thus creating new ones. This is a difficult area, which needs special sensitivity, patience and endurance. In any case, the church cannot be indifferent to this field. The word of life, freedom, justice and hope, which it continues to transfer through the centuries, has to reach, in a dynamic way, the thought and heart of its most restless children.

b) As our planet is becoming a "megalopolis" of which Christians constitute a minority -- less than one third -- the need for unity among Christians and the dialogue with people of other religious convictions are taking on new dimensions and special importance. In particular, the need for unity among all Christians is more direct and imperative. We Christians are now aware that we cannot offer our witness in a convincing manner as long as we are divided. Reconciliation and unity of Christians has direct missionary dimensions and consequences.

For the Orthodox, priority has to be given to a closer collaboration with the Ancient Churches of Africa and Asia, which lived throughout history being faithful only to the three first Ecumenical Councils. These are churches of resistance and martyrdom. Miraculously they survived, inspite of the terrible conditions they endured during several centuries. And yet, they are today fervently involved in spreading the gospel in Asia and Africa.

The last forty years have shown that we Orthodox have the possibility, and also the obligation, to contribute in a decisive way to the ecumenical quest, using the richness accumulated through twenty centuries of theological experience in various historical and social circumstances. But also, our participation in the relative conferences and consultations of the World Council of Churches has proved fruitful, not only for the others, but also for us, due to the new insights for our theological problems, new issues coming from the experience, and the successes or the mistakes of the west.

c) In the case of the religious searches, we observe not only indifference but also explosive situations. Islam and the religious systems emerging from Indian thought express their points concerning the coming new era, and so they propose interpretations and solutions. The issues of Christian mission and dialogue with people other faiths acquire new dimensions and new challenges.

In the new inter-religious dialogue, which has already begun, the Orthodox are given the opportunity to practice another kind of "Orthodox witness"; through a positive and clear unfolding of our church's theology and experience, which often helps to transcend the one-sided trends that have been developed in the thought and the ethos of the western churches. A serious study in the science of religion is to the general missionary effort what mathematics is for the growth of the physical sciences. In addition, we Orthodox, with our experience of the weaknesses and trials of the past, can counter-balance the accusation expressed towards Christianity, that it has been aggressive and colonial. We Christians of the Orthodox Churches have to give -- as a counter-weight to the pressure and the mistakes of western Christianity -- the weight of our own experience and our martyrdom in the long history of sufferings of and pressures by Muslim states and majorities (Middle East, Balkans, Egypt, Syria).

Concerning the theological understanding of non-Christian religious beliefs from an Orthodox point of view, I will confine myself to a brief exposition of the following thoughts.[13] According to biblical history, several "covenants" between God and humanity took place early in time and still keep their importance and validity. The first was made with Adam and Eve, that is, with the representatives of the whole of humankind. The second was with Noah and the new humanity who were saved from the flood (Gen. 8). The third covenant was made with Abraham (Gen. 12), the head of a race of people who were to play a basic role within God's plan for the salvation of the whole human race. The last and final, the ever "New Covenant," took place in Jesus Christ, the new Adam. But all human beings, created "in the likeness of God," are in a relation to God through a covenant that he sealed.

Acknowledging the presence of inherent important values in the religious experience of others, even spermatic word, we also admit that they possess certain possibilities for a new flourishing from within. Justin concluded his brief reference to the *logos spermaticos* with a basic principle which, strangely enough, is not stressed by those referring to his position. He emphasizes the difference between seed (*sperma*) and the realization of the fullness of the life inherent in it; and he also differentiates between inherent "force" (*dynamis*) and "grace" (*charis*). "Because a seed of something, a type given according to the inherent force, is not the same with this, through the grace of which the transformation and copying (of it) is realized" (II Apol. 13:6).

Religions are organic wholes but, as they are experienced by living human beings, they are "living wholes" in development and evolution. They have their own internal dynamism and *enteleheia.* They receive influences, absorb new ideas coming to their environment and adapt themselves to new challenges.

In view of this, Christian truths are penetrating and developing in various religious searches all over the world, through other challenges. Here, the contribution of dialogue can be decisive.

* * *

To conclude : in today's existing search by the entire human race, the Orthodox Christian experience and ethos are condensing a unique richness for humanity. Our mission is to assimilate it, to live it creatively within the new situations, in deep love with our brothers and sisters of other traditions. Always keeping our antennae sensitive to the messages that the world sends forth, or better yet, God, through the world and creation, which are his. Investigating them seriously with realism, we are called to re-estimate our position and life in a trinitarian, ecclesiological and eschatological perspective.

Mission, as everything in Orthodox life, is not only realized "in the name of the Father, and of the Son, and of the Holy Spirit," but mainly, it is a participation in the life of the Holy Trinity, an expression of this love with all the power of existence, "with all (our) hearts, and with all (our) souls, and with all (our) minds." Mission is an essential expression of Orthodox self-conscience, a cry in action for the fullfilment of God's will "on earth as it is in heaven." I would like to stress here what we have been stressing for the past twenty-five years; that indifference to mission is a denial of Orthodoxy.

Orthodox mission, internal or external, is through its nature "ecclesiastic." It cannot be understood as an individual or a group activity, separated from the body of Christ. Those who work for it, it is the church that they serve, the church that they represent; it is the life of the church that they transplant. No one is saved alone, no one offers Christ's salvation alone. We are saved within the church, we act within the church, and what we transfer is in the name of church.

All that the church possesses is for the sake of the whole world. The church radiates it and offers it, transforming all things (*ta panta*). "The whole world," "the whole creation," not only humanity, but the whole universe participates in the restoration, which has been realized by the redeeming work of Christ, and finds again its destination in glorifying God.

Mission is the extension of the love of the Trinitarian God, for the transformation of the whole world.

NOTES

1. A. Schmemann, "The Missionary Imperative in the Orthodox Tradition", in G.H. Anderson (ed.), *The Theology of the Christian Mission*, New York 1961, p. 250-257. G. Khodre, "Church and Mission", in *Porefthendes - Go Ye* 3 (1961), p. 40-42, 56-58. N. Nissiotis, The "Ecclesiological Foundation of Mission", in *The Greek Orthodox Theological Review* 8 (1962), p. 22-52. A. Yannoulatos, "Orthodoxy and Mission", in *St Vladimir's Seminary Quarterly* 8 (1964), p. 139-148. By the same author, "The Purpose and Motive of Mission - From an Orthodox Point of View", in *International Review of Mission* 54 (1965), p. 298-307. By the same author, "Initial Thoughts toward an Orthodox Foreign Mission", in *Porefthendes - Go Ye* 10 (1968), p. 19-23, 50-52. By the same author, "Mission aus der Sicht eines Orthodoxen", in *Neue Zeitschrift für Missionswissenschaft - Nouvelle Revue de science missionnaire* 26 (1970), p. 241-252. J. Meyendorff, "The Orthodox Church and Mission: Past and Present Perspectives", in *St Vladimir's Theological Quarterly* 16 (1972), p. 59-71. E. Voulgarakis, "Orthodoxe Mission", in K. Müller und Th. Sundermeier (ed.), *Lexikon Missionstheologischer Grundbegriffe*, Berlin 1987. I. Bria (ed.), *Martyria-Mission. The Witness of the Orthodox Churches Today*, Geneva, WCC, 1980. For a broader presentation of the subject and a detailed bibliography cf. J.

Stamoolis, *Eastern Orthodox Mission Theology Today*, Maryknoll, N.Y., 1986.

2. More see in our study "Byzantion ergon evangelismou" (Byzantium, Missions), in *"Threskevtike kai Ethike Enkyklopaedia"* (Encyclopaedia of Religion and Morals), vol. 4 (1964), col. 19-59. Cf. F. Dvornik, *Les Slaves, Byzance et Rome au IXe siècle*, Paris 1929. M. Lacko, *Saints Cyril and Methodius*, Rome 1963. M. Spinka, *A History of Christianity in the Balkans*, Hamden, Conn., 1968. A. Yannoulatos, "Monks and Mission in the Eastern Church during the Fourth Century", in *International Review of Mission* 58 (1969), p. 208-226. By the same author, "Les Missions des Eglises d'Orient", in Encyclopaedia Universalis, Paris, vol. 11 (1972), p. 99-102.

3. Ch. Diehl, *Les grands problèmes de l'histoire byzantine*, Paris 1943, p. 17.

4. Cf. Eu. Smirnoff, *A Short Account of the Historical Development and Present Position of Russian Orthodox Missions*, London 1903. Otis Cary, *Roman Catholic and Greek Orthodox Missions*, Vol. 1: *A History of Christianity in Japan*, New York 1909. S. Bolshakoff, *The Foreign Missions of the Russian Orthodox Church*, London 1943. J. Glazik, *Die russisch-orthodox Heidenmission seit Peter dem Grosse*, München 1954. J. Glazik, *Die Islammission der russisch-orthodoxen Kirche*, Münster 1959. A. Yannoulatos, "Orthodoxy in China", in *Porefthendes - Go Ye* 4 (1962), p. 26-30, 36-39, 52-55. By the same author, "Orthodoxy in Alaska", in *Porefthendes - Go Ye* 5 (1963), p. 14-22, 44-47. By the same author "Orthodoxy in the Land of the Rising Sun", in *Orthodoxy 1964. A Panorthodox Symposium*, Athens 1964, p. 300-319, 338-340. E. Widmer, *The Russian Ecclesiastical Mission in Peking during the Eighteenth Century*, Cambridge, Mass., 1976. P. D. Garret, *St Innocent, Apostle to America*, Crestwood, N.Y., 1979. J.J. Oleksa, "Orthodoxy in Alaska. The Spiritual History of the Kodiak Aleut People", in *St Vladimir's Theological Quarterly 25* (1981).

5. Chrysostomos Papadopoulos, " *Hoi Neomartyres*" (The New Martyrs), 2nd ed., Athens 1934. J. Perantonis, *Lexikon tôn Neomartyrôn* (Dictionary of the New Martyrs), 3 vols., Athens 1972. D. Constantelos, "The 'Neomartyrs' as Evidence for Methods and Motives Leading to Conversion and Martyrdom in the Ottoman Empire", in *The Greek Orthodox Theological Review* 23 (1978), p. 216-234.

6. The following reviews constitute an important source of information about recent developments in missionary churches. Greek and English : *Porefthentes - Go Ye*, Athens, Vol. 1 (1959) to 10 (1968), Greek : *Phôs Ethnôn*, Patras, *Exoterike Hierapostole*, Thessaloniki, *Panta Ta Ethne*,

Athens. English : *Hierapostole-Mission*, St Augustine, Fl.. Finnish : *Lähetysviesti*, Helsinki.

7. Nilus the Ascet, Homely on the Prayer 124, *Philokalia tôn hierôn neptikôn*, Athens, Vol. 1, 1957, p. 187.

8. For a good synthesis of the results of these consultations cf. Ion Bria (ed.), *Go Forth in Peace. Orthodox Perspectives on Mission*, Geneva, WCC, 1986.

9. A. Yannoulatos, "Theology, Mission and Pastoral Care", in Savas Agouridis (ed.), *Deuxième Congrès de Théologie Orthodoxe*, Athens 1978, p. 292-310.

10. Other theological aspects of the same subject have been developed in certain of my previous studies, such as: "A la redécouverte de l'ethos missionnaire de l'Eglise orthodoxe", in *Aspects de l'Orthodoxie*, Strasbourg 1978, p. 78-96; "Culture and Gospel. Some Observations from the Orthodox Tradition and Experience", in *International Review of Mission* 74 (1985), p. 185-198; "Remembering Some Basic Facts in Today's Mission", in *International Review of Mission* 77 (1988), p. 4-11.

11. Cf. Vl. Lossky, *Théologie mystique de l'Eglise d'Orient*, Paris 1944, p. 175. Engl. trans. : *The mystical Theology of the Eastern Church*, Crestwood, N.Y., 1976, p. 178.

12. D. Barret, "Annual Statistical Table on Global Mission: 1987", in *International Bulletin of Missionary Research* 11 (1987), p. 24.

13. El. Voulgarakis, "Mission and Unity form the Theological Point of View", in *International Review of Mission* 54 (1965), p. 298-307. A. Yannoulatos, "Réflections d'un Orthodoxe sur la coopération interconfessionnelle dans la Mission", in *40e Semaine de Missiologie de Louvain*, Louvain 1970, p. 101-110. J. Meyendorff, "Unity and Mission", in *Worldmission* 26 (1975), 3, p. 39-42.

14. More on this subject: L. Filippidis, *Religionsgeschichte als Heilsgeschichte in der Weltgeschichte*, Athens 1953. N. Arseniev, *Revelation of Life Eternal. An Introduction to the Christian Message*, Crestwood, N.Y., 1965. G. Khodre, "Christianity in a Pluralistic World - The Economy of the Holy Spirit", in *The Ecumenical Review* 23 (1971), p. 118-128. A. Yannoulatos, "Towards World Community", in *Ecumenical Review* 26 (1974), p. 619-636, with additions in : S.J. Samartha (ed.), "Towards a 'koinonia agapes'", *Towards World Community;* the Colombo Papers, Geneva 1975, p. 45-64. By the same author, *Various Christian Approaches to the Other Religions. A Historical Outline*, Athens 1971. By

the same author, "Emerging Perspectives on the Relationship of Christians to People of Other Faith. An Eastern Orthodox Contribution", in *International Review of Mission* 77(1988), p. 332-346. I. Karmiris, *He pankosmiotes en Christô sôterias*, (The universality of the salvation in Christ), Athens 1981.

WITNESSING TO THE GOSPEL TODAY

WITNESSING IN THE ISLAMIC CONTEXT

Fr Joseph EL-ZAHLAOUI

I belong to the Church of Antioch where the followers of Jesus of Nazareth were first called "Christians." As it is written in the Book of Acts (11:26), this church was established by the apostles, Peter and Paul.

We Christians of Antioch, like all the Christians of the Middle East, have lived the rule of the Roman, Byzantine, Arab Islamic and Ottoman empires as well as the attacks of the Crusades, and later the divisive and alienating impact of western colonialism and mission. It was a history of joy but also of deep suffering brought about by the ruling power, the religious majority, or the "schismatic" Christian groups. Despite the trials and tribulations endured during these historic periods, the church continued and played a very important role in the life of the people of this region. This miraculous historic continuation of the living faith through the power of the Holy Spirit has convinced us that the witness to the gospel in the context of the monotheistic religions (Islam and Judaism) may not be limited to the preaching of Christian principles nor to the teaching of moral values, but may go to the extent of *martyria* or the "baptism of blood."

As far as Islam is concerned, immediately after the Islamic conquest of the "fertile crescent," Damascus -- the new see of the church of Antioch -- gradually became an important centre of Islamic civilization. According to Islamic tradition, Jesus' return will occur in Damascus, where he will defeat the anti-Christ. Theology increasingly began to be expressed in the Arabic language, and Christian thought and tradition were integrated into the Arabic cultural ethos. Today my church is the church of the Arab or "arabized" Christian Orthodox. Its language is that of the Qur'an. It is therefore neither Greek nor Russian. I say this because many westerners continue to think that all Arabs are Muslims. They forget that Arab Christianity existed before Islam and that those of other cultures were arabized a long time ago, as they forget that many Muslims in the Middle East are not necessarily of Arabic origin. I remember that when I was doing my studies in Thessaloniki, I was occasionally asked by students if I was a Muslim, despite the fact that I was a deacon. Those asking the question assumed this because I spoke Arabic and came from Damascus, the capital of the Omayyads. My answer was always, "I am a Christian Orthodox from the city of St John of Damascus." And still some could never imagine that I could be Orthodox and not be Greek.

I mention this anecdote in order to remind you that Christianity has integrated into the Arabic-Islamic ethos to the extent of making Christians play an essential role in the cultural, ideological and scientific renaissance of the Arab world. Christianity became, in different periods of our history, an essential spiritual force in the cultural, social and political life of Arab Muslims. This fact deepened our belief, and despite the difficulties Christians have encountered, and are encountering today, through Islamic extremist revivalism, the witness to the gospel lies in the ability of Christians to remain an essential qualitative dimension in the life and development of the Islamic community.

Christian witness today

The vocation of the church of Jesus Christ in this world is to be the sacrament of the love of God for everyone, and to be the sign of anticipation of a new communion among men and women. This communion in the church is nurtured by the death and resurrection of Jesus, which breaks down all those walls that the human being never ceases to raise.

Thus the church, called to be a force of the Spirit in the service of a universal, "catholic" community, is open to everyone. The church must be "the house of all," where everybody feels at home. The church must be capable of recognizing the Holy Spirit at work in the lives and activities of those who do not belong to the church, whatever their culture. The eucharist within the church, as well as the sacrament and mystery of the communion, should not be seen as separated from the eucharist, which is fulfilled outside the church on the altar of the world, as St John Chrysostom so eloquently declared.

In the light of this vocation, how do Christians in the Islamic context live their faith and witness to the gospel, both in regard to and in encounter with the other?

One important factor of the current situation is the resurgence of conservative religious trends in the world, which is affecting Islam, Judaism and Christianity. In the case of Islam, Christians perceive trends towards the islamization of society. This phenomenon of islamization can be more concretely defined as the partial enforcement of *sharia*, or Islamic law, in society instead of the modern laws adopted by the modern nation states. This phenomenon is generating pressures, both actual and potential, real and imagined, thus causing fears that are exacerbated by the prevailing uncertainty with regard to the future, affecting the psychology of both the Christian minority and the Muslim majority.

The witness to the gospel challenges us to transform the prevailing destructive suspicion between the minorities and majorities into constructive confidence. As the Middle East Council of Churches' Fourth General Assembly put it, it is necessary to replace the isolating fears from each other with the hope that comes from God, which leads us to discover the signs of hope within each person and each community. We should seek to struggle together not only for the rights of any particular group, but also for the dignity of each, and above all, for the integrity of those who are victims of injustice. If our Christian faith is authentically lived, this responsibility of all people in every society, regardless of colour, race and creed, becomes a spiritual dimension, a fidelity to Christ, who calls us to assume on behalf of everybody all true human solidarity.

Another issue raised by Christians in Antioch and the Middle East in general relates to the Islamic concept of *Dhimmi.* Non-Muslims, if they are from the "religions of the Book" and live within the "abode of Islam" (*Dar El Islam*) are to be protected by the Muslims. Non-Muslims (including Christians, not living within the "abode of Islam") are part of *Dar El Harb.* When necessary, and under a certain number of conditions, holy war (*Jihad*) is permitted against them. The revival of the concept of *Dhimmi,* which does not exist in the present modern Arab constitutions, is considered by the revivalist extremist Islamic movement as the logical consequence of the restoration of the divine right and power over human beings and society.

They consider that the modern humanists, rooted in Christianity and especially the western renaissance, have boosted the right and the power of human beings at the expense of God, who was marginalized by the emerging secular society to the extent of being totally eliminated by modern atheism. This trend is to re-enter life and power in God instead of the human being. Unfortunately, although legitimate, this movement is mainly a reaction to secularism, going from extreme humanism, which killed God, to extreme theocracy, which reduces the value of or even kills the human being. This tension between God and humankind was solved when God and the human being were reconciled through the incarnation of Jesus Christ as the result of God's love for humanity and creation. The dichotomy between God and the human being, which resulted later in history from humanist philosophy and secularist theology, has been challenged by the eastern Christian concept of *theosis,* i.e., a "God in man" or "man in God" theology rooted in the reality of the incarnation.

Our witness from within monotheism, which we share with Islam and Judaism, is to encourage the return to the centrality and supremacy of God in our personal and collective life, but at the same time to challenge with courage the tendencies of monopolization, exclusivism and superiority in God's name in order to manifest the reconciliatory power of the incarnation and consequently the equality of all human beings within God's creation.

Encounter and collaboration as forms of witness

Within the framework of *Dhimma*, the marginalizing protection granted by Islam in the name of the rights of God, we experienced the encounter of religions in a very concrete way. Traditional universes are self-contained and each one explained the other by attempting to reduce it. St John of Damascus and his followers saw in Islam a Judeo-Christian heresy. Islam believed that Nicea had falsified the gospel by associating Jesus with divinity. For Islam, Jesus is indeed the "seal of Holiness," but he was considered a prophet who, most probably, was not crucified. God cannot have a son, and Christians have not understood their own scriptures; the Qur'anic revelation alone restores the truth of Christianity.

Yet at that time there were many contacts among the ordinary people in their ways of living and feeling, in their nearly identical sense of transcendence, their equal trust in providence, their same humble submission to God's will.

There were many contacts on the philosophical, scientific and technical levels, where Christians communicated the Greek heritage to the Muslims. Collaboration was never broken off; a collaboration that could be so precious nowadays in order to direct modern knowledge and power to the service of the human being, "vicar" or "image" of God.

Finally, on the level of spirituality at its highest, the similarity of Christian hesychasm and Muslim *dhikr* is striking. We even use the same rosary to invoke the divine name, and there exists the similarity between the "folly in Christ" and the "folly for God" of the Muslims.

Despite the suspicion, and even opposition, expressed by some Muslim powers in regard to theological exchange with Christians, our witness is to enable Muslim intellectuals to discover a Christianity that has no political links with the west and that often conveys familiar categories. It is of substance and flesh. It emphasizes the divine glory radiating from the risen Christ.

The invitations extended to Patriarch Elias IV and Patriarch Ignatios IV to speak at the Islamic summit in Lahore in 1974 and in Taif (Saudi Arabia) in 1980 were unique opportunities given to Antioch, as well as a challenge to fulfil this responsibility.

Witness and diakonia

Medico-social and educational services constitute a pre-eminent place of encounter with those who do not share in our religion. We carry out not only church but also national work, and we do it without ambiguities and in the very name of our faith. Most non-Christians in contact with us are well aware that our service is not a hidden means of proselytizing.

We express concern for all without distinction, however we must ask ourselves how far such an openness towards the others should be extended. Marked by our minority situation, we are often tempted to see others as being of marginal concern, since our pastoral preoccupations are centred mainly around the maintenance and defence of our flock.

The recent years of difficulty have reinforced that tendency. Numerous Christians, who once lived in openness with others, have come to lose hope and retreat into self-centredness. This phenomenon is present in different forms in our entire Middle East region. Thus non-Christians have relatively little place in our pastoral concerns and in our spiritual life as such, even though the important thing is to welcome the other, as the other, into one's own spiritual life. I must make the other a part of my own life; I must bring the other's concerns before God, make the other's concern my concern, the other's sufferings my sufferings, and feel really and truly concerned about the other.

The challenge is to *faithfully* fulfil our ministry of intercession: to intercede for somebody is to become responsible for him/her. There exists a movement of spiritual solidarity with Muslims for the purpose of "substituting" (*badal, bada-liyya*) ourselves for our brothers and sisters, and linking them to the mystery of Christ through our prayers and sufferings.

Thus, if non-Christians enter our spiritual life, we will discover that the spiritual life is the place of encounter between them and us. Such an encounter on the spiritual level can enable us to overcome certain ambiguities of a theological or human nature.

In an encounter on the spiritual level, and not just face to face, we are gathered before the living God, who is not an idea to be debated but a personal and living reality summoning us all to conversion (*tawba*) and the opening of ourselves to his thoughts, which are not our thoughts. In such a spiritual encounter, the very person of the other summons me, contributes something to me, represents to me something of God's otherness.

Obviously enough, it is not easy to reach that level of encounter. Spiritual life does not exist in isolation from belief, and dogmatic differences will have their repercussions on the spiritual level as well. In addition, the same words sometimes denote different realities. All this, however, will not prevent the spiritual dimension from offering a fundamental opening that will permit us to go beyond ideas and to turn our view towards God, who always is greater than all ideas and concepts. The spiritual dimension will also enable us to accept one another with our differences and to live these differences in mutual respect and "with God's own patience."

Such a spiritual opening towards the other must come about not only among individuals but also in our communities. This, however, presupposes that, in order for our communities to be living communities that give testimony not only through the lives of a few of their individual members but also as witnessing communities, the sociological church must become the "Holy church."

Obstacles to witness

A first obstacle to witnessing through life and expressing our Christian faith genuinely and credibly is the dualism that we very often find in religious and daily life. Too many Christians, accustomed to their situation as a minority, conceive of their religious life as being only within the church and thus reduced to certain acts of worship and religious service. They consider their public life (work, relationships, etc.) to be just a matter of survival and of getting along. Such a faith is marked by a profound dualism and will be sterile for it lacks the value of witness and does not aid non-Christians to a new understanding of the Christian experience.

Probably the major obstacle to the witness of the church is its disunity and division. Where the church should be a manifestation of God's love to all human beings and a united community in God's peace, it often appears as a gathering of sects, mutually exclusive of one another.

So it appeared to Mohammed in his era. The Qur'an (S.V. 14) says in regard to Christians, "We have aroused among them hostility and hate (*al-adawa wal-bagdaa*) till the Day of Resurrection," and this continues to be so to this day. As long as we Christians disregard the will of Christ -- "that they all be one" -- and do not become engaged in a quest for that unity, showing more faith and more confidence that the Spirit is at work in all our ecclesial communities, we shall continue to maintain that great obstacle to the witness of our faith and to the credibility of all the things we say about love and peace. True unity is not something to be directed against anybody, but is meant to be in the interest of all "so that the world may believe that you have sent me."

We often say -- and this is true -- that we do not have an adequate expression of our Christian dogma that is understandable in our context both for Christians and for those questioning. Before posing the question about the theoretical expression, however, should we not ask ourselves what the impact of this dogma is on our life? The Christian dogma becomes meaningful only when it is lived.

Thus we could ask ourselves, what is the existential sense that the dogma of the Trinity has for Christians? What role does it play in our lives?

Thus the dogma of the incarnation implies that God comes to encounter us where we are. The mystery of the humbleness of God or the mystery of the cross imply that God in Christ Jesus has vanquished injustice by assuming all the consequences thereof, and that God can be recognized in all who have become victims of injustice. Also implied is the need to pardon even those who reject us.

We should therefore ask ourselves whether we truly believe in all of these and whether we, in fact, live these mysteries. Or should we rather say that we are not capable of expressing our Christian faith because, in a way, we do not truly believe?

The issue of expressing our Christian faith is therefore an issue of life before it becomes a question of verbal expression, of discourse on faith.

Having said this, however, it is more than evident that we also face problems of verbal expression. Even when truly living these mysteries, we are still faced with the difficulty of giving expression to them in a language understandable in our context. We are faced as well with the problem of a lack of books and other works in this field that adequately and correctly respond to our cultural and religious context.

We stand in urgent need of spiritual and theological reflection on the meaning of our faith and of our beliefs in the Islamic context in which we live. This requires a solid knowledge of the whole theological tradition and a solid assimilation of the whole contemporary Arabic and Islamic cultures in order to be able to produce a correct synthesis.

The great question addressed today to our catechetical endeavours is how to discover the unique value of Christianity without making it fanatical and closed to others; how to help others to open themselves and to discover the ways of God in their religious and secular life and culture without falling into relativism and indifference. Theoretically it may sound easy to solve this dilemma. In practice, however, it is more difficult and people are exposed to two traps: fanaticism and relativism.

Conclusion

The basic requirement for witnessing to the gospel in the Islamic Arab world is through renewal in the Spirit. This should help us learn to receive others in our hearts, present ourselves before God -- who always is greater than all else -- to become engaged with God in defending human integrity and promoting a truly human society. Thus we will be able to imply ourselves in humility and challenge all powers and principalities as Jesus did, and consequently witness to the kingdom of God.

Our faith is an existential conviction before it becomes an oral or written discourse. Let us then, according to the words of the first epistle of St Peter (3:15), "be ready always to give an answer to every man who asks us for the reason of the hope that is in us, and to do so with meekness and respect, having a good conscience."

WITNESSING IN THE "SECOND WORLD"

Bishop STEFAN of Zicha

The gospel is the good news in every age and every situation, for all human beings without exception. It is always the truth of God -- divine, changeless revelation. The word of the Lord and the seed of the gospel are unchanging, but the sowing in the fields of the Lord vary, and it is therefore impossible to make a categorical definition of the ways of witness.

In the socialist countries, the so-called "second world," the circumstances of witnessing to Christ's gospel have changed radically in the majority of Orthodox churches. For the Orthodox in socialist countries, the ways of experiencing, and especially the traditional ways of witnessing to their faith, have changed.

We are faced with the question, what does it mean to witness to one's faith? Primarily this means confessing, living and proclaiming one's personal spiritual and evangelical experience. The one who does not live the gospel cannot witness to the gospel. Therefore, St John the Evangelist says: "that which we have heard, which we have seen with our eyes, which we have looked upon and touched with our hands concerning life...we proclaim to you" (I John 1:1-2).

The preaching of and witnessing to the gospel is the will of God, and is therefore the duty of every Christian: "You shall be my witnesses...to the end of the earth" (Acts 1:8). We pray daily in the Lord's prayer, "Thy will be done." This is the will of God: that all who believe in him proclaim his word and witness to it.

The most important factor is the Holy Spirit and the grace of God. The Saviour says, "You shall receive power when the

Holy Spirit has come upon you; and you shall be my witnesses" (Acts 1:8).

Orthodoxy and atheism

We come now to the question: which of the Orthodox churches exist and live in socialist countries today? They are the following: Russian, Georgian, Romanian, Serbian, Bulgarian, Polish, Czechoslovakian and Albanian. It is not possible within the scope of this survey to enter into details concerning the particular circumstances of each of these churches, thus I make reference only to the conditions under which they work and their particular engagement in witness to their Orthodox faith.

The recent history of the Russian Orthodox Church dates from 1917, when the Bolsheviks came to power. The other aforementioned Orthodox churches lived through a socialist revolution in 1944 and 1945. In the regions covered by these churches, atheism as the state religion is a common factor. Another such factor is the struggle, to a greater or lesser degree, against the church and the faith. A considerable number of related factors in the fate of some Orthodox churches are unknown to this day. Very little, rather the least, is known about the life of the Albanian Orthodox Church, which was granted autocephaly in 1937. At that time, only twenty percent of the total population of Albania were Orthodox Christians. Their agony began in 1945, and still virtually nothing is known about the life of this church.

The church of Christ has experienced and lived through great persecution, suffering and martyrdom from the very beginning of its history. These persecutions, however, were not carried out on behalf of the atheistic state systems. The persecutors were indeed the enemies of Christianity but in a different way, frequently changing not only their methods but also their fundamental approach. Marxist atheism today has a different approach to religion in general, as well as to Orthodoxy in particular. Lenin insisted that Marxist atheism must be aggressive and militant both in theory and in practice. Marxist atheism therefore became the state religion, first in the Soviet Union and then in the other lands that came under its domination and influence.

The constitution of each of these countries makes the following statement: "The church is separate from the state, and the schools from the church." But it also says: "The Party may not be neutral towards religion. It must engage in the anti-religious struggle against each and every religious superstition." These fundamental tenets have to a greater or lesser extent been put into practice, although tactics have varied. At times, the struggle has involved direct persecution of the church, and at others, use of indirect methods have been made. The Soviet constitution of 1918 permitted "freedom of religious and atheistic propaganda." In the new constitution, of 1929, however, there is change, giving "freedom of belief, and of anti-religious propaganda." The third Constitution of 1936, provides only "freedom of worship, and of anti-religious propaganda." What does this mean? Freedom to worship, but restriction of all other missionary activity by the church. These tactics against the churches of Russia and Georgia were continued against the other Orthodox churches living under Marxist domination.

What were these tactics? One can give a general reply. The churches were persecuted in various ways: by the murder, imprisonment and exile of bishops, priests and laity; the forbidding of religious instruction starting from kindergarten to the university; the terrorizing of believers; the closing down of monasteries, churches and theological colleges; the shutting down of church publishing houses and so forth, not to mention the day-by-day anti-religious propaganda through all possible channels: the press, films, plays, radio, etc.

Obviously, the situation was not the same for all Orthodox churches. Even within one country, the situation could vary from region to region. Within the area covered by the Serbian Orthodox Church, there are dioceses where things have been considerably more difficult, and others where life has been much easier. The steam-roller of atheism in the postwar years left an infinitely deeper impression on those parts of the Serbian Orthodox Church where the Ustashi terror during World War II had destroyed almost eighty percent of the churches and massacred more than fifty percent of the faithful. In other regions, where the situation was easier during the war, the church's resistance was more successful. Here, other internal factors came into question: nationalist, political, socio-economic, local customs, traditions, etc. It is true that many fell away from the church, succumbing to the weight of temptation. On the other hand, there were those who experienced the rich outpouring of the grace of God through supernatural events.

Recently the situation has changed considerably. It is true that Lenin created a dictatorship of the proletariat, but there is virtually no state in which the workers have continued to hold power: the proletariat has been transformed into a ruling elite. Marxism was revolutionary while it struggled for power; when it achieved power, it became conservative. Defending its power, it has convulsively reigned on those who seek change. This is evident today and is the main spur to change in socialist countries where the state's attitude to religion and to the church are in question. Many Christians are dissatisfied with capitalism, as are a number of Marxists dissatisfied with the bureaucratic outlook of their leaders. This is the main reason for the infinitely tolerant attitude towards religion in general. In many socialist countries, the present situation and conditions make it much more possible for the Orthodox churches to fulfil their obligation and duty of witness to the gospel of Christ.

One of our Yugoslav specialists in Marxism recently wrote, "Theism and atheism are like the two sides of a coin." In our country it is now possible to read in the press some encouraging news of the life and work of the church. Our largest church is in the process of being built in Belgrade, and will be dedicated as a memorial to St Savas, the greatest father of our church and our people. A considerable number of declared atheists have contributed towards the building of this church. It is no longer an unusual event for public debates between believers and non-believers to be organized in our country.

A further point: In socialist states, statistics of the numbers of believers and non-believers are frequently produced. These numbers, however, are never realistic. Atheists very frequently come secretly to the church seeking baptism either for themselves or their children. We know of many occasions where they seek the prayers of the church. This is a sort of modern "catacomb" in the life of the Orthodox Church.

Modes of witness

1. *Liturgical life*

One of the first bishops of the Russian Orthodox Church to visit Europe after the war was asked: "What do you do in the Orthodox Church in Russia under the present circumstances?" He replied: "We celebrate the liturgy." Not only in the Russian Orthodox Church but in all Orthodox churches under socialism, the divine liturgy and church services in general are the greatest factors in witnessing to the Christian faith.

In the history of the Orthodox churches, from the earliest times there have been periods when church services have been the only possible public form and expression of church life. These have been periods where Christian schools and theological colleges were not found, without publications or books and sometimes without the public preaching of the gospel. The church mainly preserved the faith among its people solely through church services. Orthodox liturgy in itself contains inexhaustible spiritual power and great catechetical richness. This was especially confirmed in the periods of oppression by the Turks in the Balkans, and is the case under any non-Christian people.

This was the situation and to some degree remains so to the present day in countries in which the state has imposed a totalitarian, anti-religious ideology and reduced the life of the Orthodox Church to the "practice of a cult." The altar and the holy eucharist have been the one spiritual school, pulpit and gathering place of the ecclesial and national community.

This situation has called the Orthodox churches to diligence in the nurturing of liturgical celebration, and especially to a recognition of the importance of the vernacular in services.

From the beginning, side by side with the liturgy, holy icons have played a particular missionary role. In the ancient Christian catacombs, symbolic figures were portrayed on the walls. They secretly depicted people and events in the history of the church which witnessed the truths of the faith to the first Christians and at the same time hid the divine mysteries from pagans and pantheists. It is known that in Orthodox churches holy icons were venerated and that iconography was cherished as an important form of spiritual life. In the present-day circumstances of Orthodox churches that are more-or-less restricted in their missionary and catechetical activity, the use of holy icons in the church and at home have greater meaning than ever in the past. This is confirmed by the mass of Orthodox believers who stream into our monasteries and churches, which are decorated with precious frescoes and icons. The holy figures and events are experienced as a window through which heaven looks on earth, and heavenly realities can be seen from earth.

2. *The witness of the martyrs*

Long ago, St John the Divine had a vision, which he described as such: "Then I saw thrones, and seated on them were those to whom judgement was committed; also I saw the souls of those who had been beheaded for their testimony of Jesus and for the word of God, and who had not worshipped the beast or its image and had not received its mark on their foreheads or their hands." (Rev. 20:4). Of all forms of witness by which a human being can testify to his/her faith, the voices of those who have laid down their lives in proclaiming the word of God are heard the most clearly.

A historian has written that during the great persecutions of Christians in the early centuries, about forty million in all perished. An incomparably greater number of Christians have suffered in the last sixty-five years. It is held that under Stalinist terror in the Soviet Union alone, about sixty million people suffered. There is documented evidence that in one concentration camp in Yugoslavia, Jasenovac, approximately one million people were martyred between 1941 and 1945, ninety percent of them were Serbs. The main reason for their massacre at the hands of the Croatian Ustashe was that they were Orthodox believers. This was only one of ninety such places of execution in which Orthodox Serbs suffered during the last war.

It is difficult to provide statistics on the number of martyrs in the remaining Orthodox churches in the countries of the so-called "second world" who have also sacrificed their lives "for the witness of Jesus and for the word of God." This witness will endure for all time, not only within Orthodoxy but in the whole Christian world, as most precious pearls in the treasury of Christianity.

One of our poets has written that their graves are not tombs, but "cradles of new strength." This is precisely what they are within Orthodoxy today.

Fedotov, in his book, "A Treasury of Russian Spirituality," makes reference to the words of Archpriest Avakum: "Satan succeeded in dyeing our God-enlightened Russia with the blood of the martyrs." This innocent blood cries out to heaven, and neither time nor the elements will be able to wipe it out. As St John the Divine says: "The devil is about to throw some of you into prison, that you may be tested" (Rev. 2:10). Even so, Satan will never in the last resort be the victor.

3. *The witness of churches and monasteries*

Speaking about the significance of the house of God, the Psalmist says: "Thy testimonies are very sure; holiness becometh Thy house, O Lord, for ever" (Psalm 92/3:5). In Orthodox churches found in certain socialist countries, a great number of churches have been destroyed, and others used for secular purposes. In other countries, churches were destroyed by the invaders during the last war. This was the case in three of our dioceses in Yugoslavia, where the Ustashe destroyed and burned down about eighty percent of the churches. Many of these churches were restored in the postwar years, others, however, are still in ruins and await restoration. In Orthodoxy, the church building is a holy place, which does not cease to exist in the popular consciousness even when in ruins. One of our monks from the Holy Mountain, who visited Russia, gives us a lovely example of this. He beheld a strange sight in a wheatfield. A young couple stood there: the young man in his best clothes and the girl in a wedding gown. They were making the sign of the cross with great frequency and were singing a hymn. The monk drew near to see what was happening, and learned that there had been a church there, but it had been pulled down. The young man had taken his bride there for God to crown their marriage with his blessing because there was no church or priest in the area.

Within the diocese entrusted to me, that of Zicha, the occupiers destroyed a number of churches during the last war. In the places that have not yet been rebuilt, the people gather from time to time for prayer on the site of the former church. This takes place especially on the day of the church's patronal feast. On one occasion, I celebrated vespers on one such site. A man who had been present wrote about the event in one of our papers under the heading: "Service in a non-existent church." In a most touching article, he wrote of how the Orthodox people prayed with fervour in a church that existed only in their souls, since it had been razed to its foundations forty-five years earlier.

In some Orthodox churches in socialist countries, monasteries have been closed, turned into museums or even into centres of atheist propaganda. Over against this, however, the desire for monasticism has unexpectedly grown. Anyone who has visited one or another of the monasteries of the Orthodox Church in Russia will verify this.

Recently in an American journal there appeared an article entitled: "A candle that never burns out," about the visit to Moscow this year of Margaret Thatcher, Prime Minister of Great Britain. She obviously went for political reasons, but her religious awareness led her to visit the monastery of the Holy Trinity and St Sergius at Zagorsk. She bowed low before the coffin of St Sergius of Radonezh and lit a large candle. "They endured, and they were the victors," said this stateswoman, who much ressembles one of her great predecessors, Gladstone. The monasteries have indeed remained through the centuries "candles that never burn out" for all Orthodox Christians.

4. *The witness of the Orthodox family*

In all Christian churches, the family is of fundamental importance in witnessing to faith. The Holy Apostle Paul called the Christian family "the house church," and St John Chrysostom "the little church." The educative role of the family is especially significant in the Orthodox churches where for decades there has been no Christian education outside the home and family. A vital role was and is played by the parents, with the influence of the mother being the most important. In many cases, the grandmother has replaced the mother, especially in families where the mother goes out to work. We can indeed quote the words of the Old Testament: "As the sun shineth upon the mountains of the Lord, so is the example of a virtuous woman in the ordering of her house" (Sirach/Eccles. 26:16).

The conditions for raising children and education are in crisis throughout the entire world. You can imagine what it is like in countries where religious and moral education are forbidden. Not long ago an article appeared in our press entitled, "Trials of the crucified generation." Our younger generation is indeed crucified on the cross between school and church, the home and the streets, parents and teachers, divisions to the right and to the left, consciousness and unconsciousness.

In such situations, the family and the church are confronted by an extremely difficult task and responsibility. In the church, the example of the priest is paramount, and in the Christian family, that of the parents. One of the greatest educators of the world often said: "Example, example, and again I say to you: example!"

In the last few years, there has been in our country a great influx of young people into the churches. Groups of students often come for baptism and most frequently to the monasteries. They seek the help of an experienced spiritual guide, generally a priest-monk. In our clergy meetings today, the question that is most often posed is how the challenge of this return to the church can be met. It seems to me that this is taking place in other similarly-placed Orthodox churches and in the world as a whole.

"Strange and inexplicable are the ways of the Lord." These words were written by a young and very gifted writer of ours who had earlier been an atheist. How had he become a Christian? He says: "While drinking water from broken cisterns, I sensed their incapacity to hold water. While taking part in pagan rites of deification, I was never able to accept that the Lord was Caesar. I was brought up short in the midst of my schooling, my superficial youth, my immature view of the world and of life, and so forth. And today? Today, everything draws me to Him (God) who is Alpha and Omega."

A great number of such intellectuals, who had been declared atheists, very frequently come to the church as new members or as returning sons and daughters.

We have not spoken here of the episcopate, the clergy, the monks and nuns, church education, publications and sermons and other factors that are engaged in witnessing to the word of God in the circumstances of the Orthodox Church in socialist lands. We will cite once more the words of our young writer, "Strange and inexplicable are the ways of the Lord!" adding, "and his ways are very diverse, in these his fields of life and in the varying circumstances of our day."

In general, one could say that in all that has happened, the greatest factor has been the grace of God. In the course of the last decades of the life of the Orthodox churches and in the difficult situations referred to, much that was possible to destroy was destroyed. But all that true Christians could build within their own souls remained untouched. This was built over a long period and it is the most important witness. Children were wrested from their parents' arms, monasteries and churches were closed. Schools, libraries, spiritual and cultural wealth were appropriated, as were church goods and lands. But that which the devout could preserve in their hearts remained; it was preserved in every Orthodox church that was subjected to these great trials.

WITNESSING IN A SECULARIZED SOCIETY

Prof. Olivier CLEMENT

INTRODUCTION: IS ONE TO SPEAK OF "SECULARIZATION?"

The notion of secularization corresponds more to reality in those societies where this process is underway, such as Greek society. On the contrary, in most western societies, and in France in particular (I shall speak mainly on the basis of French experience), the problem today appears to have been left behind; for neither society nor culture are defined any longer with reference to a religious element, against a locally predominant religion. It would be better to speak of an already secularized society in search of itself.

I. WHAT IS SECULARIZATION ?

a) A summary description

We are witnessing an emancipation, an autonomization of the various spheres of existence: political, social, cultural, with regard to the Christian experience. Science, technology, know-how, arts, state authority and economic life take place outside the specifically Christian sphere. There is, therefore, neither a dominant authority nor a dominant ideology, but independent authorities, each one in its own field. The state does not claim to govern church affairs, nor the church state affairs. Science and philosophy are no more the "handmaids" of theology, which nobody is in fact preventing from developing freely. There can be several independent approaches, sometimes rivaling, to one and the same reality, not operating under the same rules.

So it is possible to speak of secularized culture as of a multiple culture, heterogeneous, typically non-totalitarian. It is no longer possible to achieve a hierarchy of knowledge in a unified and authoritative system. Every piece of knowledge, every approach to reality, is dependent on its own norms. From this standpoint, a religion that would claim to impose its dictates on the whole of politics, social and cultural life, would appear as intolerably repressive.

Such would seem to be our modern world, essentially self-critical, forever unsure of its bases as of its conquests, always in a state of ferment, kneaded by incongruous elements that are both a source of tension and the secret of its conquering strength.

Auschwitz, gulags and "demaoïzation" have killed off the great mythologies of politics and history. Criticism of these mythologies is disappearing in its turn. Economic crisis and malaise, at times the third world catastrophe, have turned to derision the philosophies of desire, which exalted the "sub-Freudianism," diffuse, of the "civilization of consumerism." The rediscovery of the human being as subject has gradually worn away the scientific structuralism which had boasted of alienating the human being from knowledge of him/herself, even and first of all in the sciences called human. The intelligentsia has at last emerged from an era of dogmatic arrogance; Solzhenitsyn has succeeded in liberating it from all totalitarian nostalgia. It is possible to speak, seek and question, without being banished to the fringe or depreciated -- even, I would say with a touch of black humour, if one is a Christian! Art is busy exploring the limits of the human condition, bringing to light anxiety, madness, the cry *de profundis*, but also a sort of poetry of perception, perhaps soon of the human countenance (celebrated in such moving terms by Levinas' philosophy). A new type of science is emerging. Such things as uniqueness, originality and problematics are being reintroduced into a study of the universe, notably in biology. In the approach to the human being, the use of narrative is rehabilitated, "demythologization" gives way to a fervent exploration of myths, not only in their functioning but also in their significance, their meaning. It is true that neo-positivism is still flourishing, but "scientism" itself has to embrace the para-normal -- a different approach to the corporal imported in particular by the Far Eastern types of medecine. I could sum up this development by simply saying that everything is henceforth an open question.

b) Origins

Secularization is an historical process, lengthy and complex, in which one can, however, discern two fundamental factors:

1. *The prevalence of instrumental reasoning*, which dates back, not to the Renaissance -- marked by a cosmic religiousness -- but to the second half of the seventeenth century. Instrumental reasoning not only wants to know the relationship of things -- as did ancient thought in its dependence on speculative reasoning -- but also wants to put it to use. Not only to know nature but to transform it, to claim mastery over it. Thus there is implied a new relationship to reality, which Max Weber describes as a "disenchantment of the world." The enchanted world is one that is bathed in mystery, such as the body as the "temple of the Holy Spirit." The disenchanted world is one in which the mechanics are laid bare: the body under the surgeon's knife.

2. *The biblical, Judeo-Christian tradition*, which has allowed the passage from Greek rationalism, seeking to discover and contemplate the order of the universe, to experimental and instrumental reasoning.

Judaism paved the way for the disenchantment of the world through the Genesis narrative of creation, and through the struggle of the prophets against idolatry. God creates all things through his word. He is not submerged in a sacred form of nature or prostitution, or in sexual ecstacy. An infinite distance is introduced between the created and the uncreated. The autonomy and specific consistency of what is real is affirmed and strengthened. It is entrusted to the responsibility of humankind which, in subjecting nature to itself, according to God's order, does not become a rival to the latter but shows forth his image. When Jesus says, "My Kingdom is not of this world" and "Give to Caesar that which belongs to Caesar and to God that which belongs to God," he is freeing the secular field from an immediate engulfing in the religious field; he is opening up a breathing space for the spirit. Marcel Gauchet, in his book whose title is borrowed from Weber and is *The Disenchantment of the World*, remarks on the following facts:

- that the paradoxical transcendence of God, as revealed in the mystery of the Cross, serves as the ground for humankind's freedom;
- that transcendence, while remaining such, nevertheless according to the doctrine of the Incarnation, allows itself to become visible in a human face, and thus ultimately in every human face. Becoming the neighbour of every human being is the best way of serving the Father.

Thus secularization is a daughter of both Athens and Jerusalem, of the contemplation of the cosmic order and of the free service of brothers and sisters. That is why Christianity should not be afraid of secularization: it can understand it from within and perhaps preserve it from its exaggerations and orientate it in another direction.

c) Effects

Secularization is here to stay: it is a transforming of the relationship of human beings to reality. Its beneficial effects are clear. Having torn itself away from a clerical stranglehold, society has done some prodigious exploring, ranging from the quark to the quasar, and some prodigious creating too -- the most remarkable being, without doubt, western music, the exploration of the cosmos, on the one hand, and of humanity on the other. In spite of setbacks, the human lifespan has been extended and the number of human beings has multiplied. The planet is being unified. Western culture is an open culture, with a tendency to recapitulate all others, all the arts, all the myths. Its implicit philosophy is *a philosophy of the other*, accepted in his otherness. Politically speaking, secularization is linked to democracy: nobody has the right to impose his/her personal truth; there is no state ideology, the state being unable to aspire to total knowledge.

Nevertheless, secularization also has ambiguous and terrifying effects. A consumer type of civilization is helping to turn the third world into a proletariat. At a time when it is taking upon itself all the experiences of human time and space, western culture is upsetting the structure of other cultures, and finally its own heritage. The development of instrumental reasoning is chopping to pieces the great symbolic references, whether it be the man-woman relationship (here the de-structuring is evidenced by the banalizing of homosexuality) or the father-son relationship (seen in nostalgia for incest).

It is a fact that the great religious institutions, the churches, are hard pressed by secularization and the loss of symbolical references. Yet there is evidence that experimental reasoning cannot answer the deep questionings of life, death, love and beauty. Thus there ensues *an ambiguous return of the religious element*. It is no longer the gross sacred awareness of the masses, of the totalitarian regimes, but an awareness of the sacred which passes itself off as spiritual, that of eclectics and sects. There is the hyper-individualism of the "spiritualities" of Californian origin, intent on "outreach" or on "breaking out." There is the delirium of fusion offered by sects and mystiques of self-dissolving, where one can escape from oneself by letting oneself be swallowed up in the quagmire of the group or the ocean of the divine. There are "the vibes." Reincarnation, strangely enough, is transposed into a reassuring individual voyage, whereas in India or in Buddhism nobody transmigrates (except, for India, the Absolute playing with himself) and that the "wheel of existence" is in fact a wheel of illusions.

Midinettes, scientists and politicians alike consult clairvoyants and astrologers.

This resurfacing of the religious instinct, however bizarre the forms it takes, has three main, stable characteristics: it is a "scientism" of the invisible, a negation of the person, a revolt against a degenerate Christianity. Experiences are all methodically worked out according to a "science" of inner awareness where there is no risk of the leap of faith and the assuming of one's personal existence, with its limits and its responsibilities. The major themes are eros and the cosmos -- as if the great battle between eros and Christ were to end with the victory of eros, an eros that thus becomes mechanical and meaningless.

II. CHRISTIANITY IN A SECULARIZED SOCIETY

Secularization eliminates a certain type of Christian presence, that of domination, of an authoritarian unification under the aegis of faith, controlling all things. Ultra-conservatives dream of a return to this type of presence, and, in a country such as France, there is a danger of Orthodoxy becoming the refuge of ultra-conservative Catholics (and also of frequently "Guenonian" Gnostics), for whom Mons. Lefebvre has not gone far enough! But there is another form of presence, of relationship to secularized society: that of a *prophetic partnership*, which is much closer to the gospel line of conduct. Today the nucleus of spiritual energy, which burst out into modernism, is well-nigh exhausted. Christians can, using humble forces, awaken a certain meaning, a certain fire, a certain light. If they do not do so, if they are unable to find their place in a secularized society, this place will be taken by the pseudo-religions I mentioned earlier.

How can the Christian faith be present in this society? My reply is the following: (a) by promoting a sense of the gratuitous, the non-assimilable; (b) by placing themselves on the level of ultimate legitimacy; (c) through a certain visibility.

a) By promoting a sense of the gratuitous, the non-assimilable

In a society where everything is interchangeable, there is a danger of everything's becoming uniform; the smallest difference is perceived as a sign of inequality, so differences must be abolished. If everything is equally valid, nothing is really important; mockery and indifference are the outcome. Today, the greatest challenge to the churches is not atheism but indifference.

If religion is to be meaningful in modern society, it has to develop a sense of the gratuitious, the non-assimilable. In her book *Enracinement* (Finding one's roots), Simone Weil attacks a form of education in which everything can be absorbed, assimilated, reduced and rendered banal; such an education, she says, runs the risk of snuffing out the spark of energy in humankind. On the contrary, a true education is one that places the human being before the irreducible, that which cannot be harnessed but which sheds light on all things, that which is gratuitous, that which is beautiful. Religion does just that: it leads us into the presence of a gratuitous, illuminating both hidden and revealed reality -- a reality that is to be contemplated, not assimilated. It is here that the religious factor acts as a powerful anthropological and social lever. It presents us not with a useful and consumable God, but with a gratuitious God who, as a result, is a source of salvation. It reaffirms the purpose of existence as being one of celebration, as being a festival.

There is no need to dwell on the crisis of language in our society of promotional palavers, of political jargon, of omnipresent and obsessional images. For Orthodoxy, liturgical praise, in which the heart awakes, and sainthood as the only true freedom -- the freedom to love truly -- are basic theological tenets, where language is continually renewed. Is not witnessing to resurrection through liturgical festivity and through the joy and compassion that shine forth from a spiritualized person the only way to cure mockery and indifference at their root?

Here, however, many problems face our church, without doubt the very opposite of those known to the western confessions. Is it not tempting to objectivize and immobilize the liturgical word, where the cross sometimes appears as the totem of the Christian empire -- a liturgical word otherwise admirable, but where certain passages fossilize the ordered world of the Constantinian era? Thus, I repeat, the Orthodox Church in the west is in danger of serving as a refuge for those who see in history only decadence, and only evil in modernization.

But beyond this inertia there remains the basic testimony; for it corresponds, I believe, to present-day humankind's deepest longing: the testimony of *beauty*. As proof, it suffices to mention the growing importance of icons, present everywhere today in France, even on the front page of provincial newspapers at Christmas and Easter; an aesthetic approach to them becomes, willy-nilly, a spiritual approach. Icons, faces whose beauty is no longer that of seduction or possession but that of communion, deathless beauty finally freed from anguish to become the torn-aside veil of love.

Of course, a desire for religion needs to be awakened by the proposition: "How are they to hear the message if no one proclaims it?" as St Paul asks (Rom. 10:14). A proposition inseparable today from freedom: "If you want to come to me, come, follow me." The proposition is presented under the sign of gratuity. One freedom calls to another.

b) By placing themselves on the level of ultimate legitimacy

1) *Our society is in search of a set of ethics*, with the dual aim of limiting the political totalitarianism of yesterday and the technological totalitarianism of tomorrow. But it has lost its unanimity on the ends pursued by human action. Hence the moral turmoil stirred up in it every time it is called upon to resolve certain fundamental issues. This is particularly evident

today in the field of bioethics. Abortion is technically possible without the slightest risk. In the name of what is one to permit it, limit it or forbid it? The serious illnesses or heavy handicaps from which the individual will suffer are foreseeable already at the embryonic stage. In the name of what is one to decide on the destruction or the preservation of the embryo? What about fertilization *in vitro* for women, married or otherwise? And surrogate mothers, etc.?

Obviously the church does not have ready-made answers to all the questions. It should not lay down the law without making sure that the existential effects of such prohibitions are understood. But it can make society take heed and remind it of the meaning of love, of the mystery of the child. It can put it on its guard against technocratic fatality, leading to barbarity, by considering everything technically possible as having to be carried out. It must remind our society that it is a society not without ethical traditions: that the Jewish, Greek, Christian tradition has modelled our understanding of the person. Doubtless it is up to Christians, backed by their church, to give an example of a stable, peaceful family life.

2) On a more profound level, the problem is one of *the very legitimacy of existence*. "I am killing myself because life has no meaning," write students. It is true that evil is blatant in injustice, oppression, deception and collective hypnoses. Everything possible must be done to reduce and limit it. Still we discover more and more that the material of which existence is woven is not only crumpled -- a thing that could be put to rights with the hot iron of human recipes -- but hopelessly torn. This tear gives rise to nihilism, a refusal of all ideologies, where one holds fast to lowly and precarious sources of happiness.

This is where we ask: does this tear open up vistas of nothingness -- or of love? Here Christians bear their testimony: evil makes us understand that we are not only of this world, but that God reaches out to us even in evil in order to turn us into resurrectional beings. Filled with the confidence and strength such a belief bestows, the person of faith struggles without losing heart against all forms of death in culture and in society. The human being maintains its irreducible character and its ontology as love; multiplies the ecclesial communities like a contagion of communion; develops a renewed reflection on the necessary liberations -- forever partial and to be undertaken again and again -- by setting out from this fundamental liberation. And simultaneously on "human rights," in a bond of friendship with all who respect the enigma of the person. The person of faith dares to say that the beyond breaks through the finite and awakens in this world seemingly closed in on itself a power for good, a life unmingled with death, a love unmingled with hate. Faith becomes *a blessing on life.* And it is without doubt of this benediction that our society stands in greatest need.

3) *Inasmuch as the state is involved*, Christians need to "debunk" it, to enlarge the sphere of liberty. The role of religion is not to seek to dominate the state, but to oblige it to limit itself to carrying out its proper function and not to overstep the mark. The state's function -- here we echo the words of Soloviev -- is not to transform society into a paradise, but to prevent its becoming hell. The limits of the state are to be found, on the one hand, in the vigour of civilian society, where it has a duty to reduce violence as much as possible and to ensure the right of free association and, on the other hand, in the great moral and spiritual institutions, which it must respect, while ensuring complete freedom of conscience.

Against a secularism that marginalizes the church and makes of religion a purely private affair, Christians have to encourage an authentic pluralism where the churches -- and also Judaism and Islam -- have their place as recognized partners whose advice is sought. In a truly pluralistic society, the Bible will be heard in schools -- or else our cultural heritage will become unintelligible to our youngsters -- and the voice of the church fathers will be heard in a study of thought. The state no longer has to protect itself from a militant clericalism, as was the case yesterday; it can recognize that religions have a social and educative function. It is a sign of the times that Christians are present, in France, on the National Board of Ethics, called upon to give their views to the legislator on moral questions arising from the development of science and technology.

So it is that secularized society, while marking the end of clericalism, can become for the churches a place where they can act as a disinterested, shining light, a place both fruitful and perilous -- for the partnership, in order to be prophetic, can become insurrectional. May Christians, renouncing power and violence, become the poor and peaceful servants of the crucified God who institutes the freedom of the person! May they be guarantors of the faith of others, guarantors, too, of those who lack faith but create -- often very humbly -- beauty and goodness! May they be the guardians of an open humanity in an open culture! All this while quietly maintaining -- *and because they maintain* -- that Christ is the victor for all over death and hell; that every person bears within him/herself the whole of humanity and thus is unique; that the church is the chalice from which there flows, "for the life of the world," the joy of the resurrection.

c) A certain visibility

It is essential that the Christian faith become a social symbol. For it is a religion of incarnation, of the Invisible made flesh who beckons. In a country such as France, where the Orthodox church is a small minority, there is a temptation to lie low: I am thinking, for example, of the numerous little Russian churches in Paris created by emigrés, between the two world wars, in garages and workshops. Moving but insufficient manifestations! The great embassy churches in Paris, or of seasonal sojourns on the Côte d'Azur for example, are dead symbols, if not misleading ones. On the contrary, certain recent buildings bear both a sure Orthodox witness and blend harmoniously with the French urban or rural scene: such are the Moulin de Senlis church at Montgeron, the little monastery of Mesnil-St-Denis in the Rambouillet forest, the church of the Centre St-Irénée in Marseille: in these three places one sees icons and frescoes of great beauty, before which one can bring a friend, a seeker of God, and say to him or her: "Come and see." Other places, like the Institut St-Serge, sensibly unite an extremely lovely church with academic buildings. This is a strong witness before the students of correspondence courses when they come to the institute, once a term, for a weekend of exams, liturgical life, reflection and friendship.

It is important that there should be "signs" in the mass media, as is the case in France, where there are Orthodox broadcasts on radio and television. Our society is greedy for "signs," but these wear out with use. So, from time to time, a new "sign" is almost inevitably ecumenical, with the Orthodox joining hands with Catholics and Protestants (here I am not thinking of purely ecumenical events, which are inter-Christian, but of events aiming to be a "sign" for the world).

Let me give you three examples. The first is the Way of the Cross improvised this year on the Champs-Elysées: thousands of Christians carrying a cross on Paris' most elegant avenue, one of the richest in the world. Depending on the building they were passing, journalists, artists and immigrants took up the cross. "Cross of the lack of work and closing doors. Cross of moral and material misery," the crowd shouted before the offices of a luxury magazine. Here, before the shop window of a famous couturier, a text of Mother Theresa is read, which alludes to "those human beings on the pavement who have lived like animals but who aspire to die like angels." "Jesus needs your hand to wipe their faces."

A second example: at Marseille, when the dates of the western and the eastern Easter coincide, representatives of the Catholic Church, the Reformed Church and the Orthodox Church climb into a boat in the Old Port and, reading in turn from the gospel, proclaim the resurrection to the crowd gathered there.

My third example is but a project, yet I would be very happy if it were carried out, for it was initiated by Orthodox believers; Russians of the third emigration, especially writers and artists, are hoping, in order to celebrate the Millenium of the Baptism of their country, to organize a *happening* on the banks of the River Seine. Just as at Kiev, in 988, the pagan idols, starting with that of Perun, the god of thunder and warriors, were thrown into the Dniepr, so the symbols of contemporary idols -- money, the "grande bouffe" (luxury foods), eroticism, violence, drugs, cars, television sets, lulling politics and obsessive publicity -- would be flung into the Seine, accompanied by baptismal chants.

Much flexibility is required in order to keep the "signs" meaningful. That is, they must constantly be referred to Christ, who beckons through "signs."

III. THEOLOGICAL TASKS

a) The first problem: approaches to the message, the possibility of rendering it intelligible to our contemporaries. In other words: "*pre-comprehension*" *of the message.*

The "signs" used during the heyday of Christendom -- a "pedagogy of fear," explaining evil as God's punishment, proof through unanimity ("Christianity is true because everybody is Christian, even the Emperor," St Athanasius was wont to say) -- are no longer meaningful.

From where is one to start, except from humankind itself? The human being as an enigma, open to the mystery of being through the frontier situations of love, beauty and death.

In several Orthodox countries in eastern Europe, an amazing experience has taken place in our century. Neither the brain-washing efforts of propaganda nor the concentration camps, nor the special psychiatric hospitals have succeeded in breaking the human spirit. There has been no surrender. People remain not only capable of dignity, but of unselfish kindness. More discreetly, the same has been taking place in western society: more numerous than one would have thought are those who do not give in to the idols of money, consumerism, success or hedonism; those who seek silence, a place of retreat, friendship, contact with nature. Thus humankind appears to be irreducible. Why? Is it not around this point that we should propose -- in a lively and concrete manner, etching "in depth," one could say -- the theme of the *image of God*?

Secularized society is a society where there most frequently reigns silence about God. In many circles it is now considered improper, almost obscene, to talk about God. It has been said that bashfulness concerning God has replaced bashfulness about sex. More than just bashfulness: a genuine inhibition. It is what our ascetics call "forgetfulness" -- a sort of slumber of the spirit that can be very agitated, and which the techniques of the mass medias fill, during moments of repose, with prefabricated dreams.

In this heavy silence, the believer's attitude is surely to refuse to make an ideology out of faith, but to become different, in a humble way, so as to have it understood that the void does not have the last word; it is especially -- to echo a phrase of Kierkegaard -- to try to "deepen people in their existence" through an authentic culture. In a word, one must *awaken* them, both to anguish and to wonder, and to existence as a question mark. When I taught history in a large Parisian college, in dealing with the nineteenth century I tried to speak with the same passion of Marx, Nietzsche and Dostoyevsky. I did not draw any conclusions. I was bound by the lay character of the institution. But frequently it happened that pupils would come and find me before or after class to have a face-to-face discussion on fundamental questions.

The ultimate approach to mystery is freedom. One must not be afraid of this demand for freedom, which is fermenting in secularized society and causing it to rear up against the last lingering traces of clericalism. This demand must be pushed to its conclusion, to rebellion against death, which opens the gate to revelation; to the desire to escape from all slavery, which opens the gate to holiness.

Thus, bit by bit, silence becomes a sort of negative theology, from which there springs a word that respects the bounds of modesty but refuses to be muzzled; that respects suffering but allows a ray of light to pass through. Far from being a scholastic elucubration of reason, it is a word of humble strength and communion beauty. A word through the silence, through pain; a word of joy and of freedom. It is the cry of Dimitri Karamazov: "If God is banished from the earth, we shall meet him beneath the earth!...Then we, the subterranean people, shall intone in the bowels of the earth a tragic hymn to the God of joy. Long live God and his joy! I love him!"

b) Second problem: on which points of the message should we insist today?

Have we dug sufficiently deep, while avoiding the treatises on God's justice of "Job's friends," into the poignant reality of radical evil? Do we know how to bring into harmony, without overdoing it, a theological and scientific reading of creation, the former telling us of a paradisial condition and of a drama prior to the present conditions of cosmic life, the latter telling us that death existed already billions of years before humankind's advent on earth? Have we sufficiently overcome the opposition between a "theology of glory," which puts to rights a bit too hastily the upside-down world of the Beatitudes and a "theology of cross," which sometimes forgets the resurrection? Should not one identify them? And rectify the traditional expressions concerning God's might without falling into an extreme "kenotism," which can only stir up the defunct theologies of the "death of God"? If the incarnate word comes into his own absence, that is, in death and hell, if the "One of the Holy Trinity" -- as Byzantine liturgy says -- dies, in his humanity, on the cross, it is in order to be resurrected and to resurrect us, to fill all things with his light. Have we really shown that the cross is not an expiatory sacrifice offered by the Son to his Father, but a sacrifice of reinstatement, sanctification and the instilling of life? Can we harmonize these two certainties: that Christ is an historic person -- which allows us to represent him in icons -- and also that he most realistically "recapitulates" in himself humanity and the universe, dragging them away from separateness in order to unite them with his Father in the Holy Spirit? In the same order of things: have we sufficiently stressed the fact that the resurrection of Jesus is not the resuscitating of a corpse into the conditions of this world, but the overthrowing of these conditions, the beginning of a transfiguration of matter, time and space?

Societies in which everything is sacrosanct have, no doubt, too long taken God's part against humankind's. All this imagery is crumbling away today thanks to the purifying atheism of men like Marx, Nietzsche, Freud, and those who followed in their wake. An imagery portraying an imperious God, a sort of policeman or celestial spy, a castrating father, a sadistic tyrant pronouncing indictments, "religion" reduced to a repressive morality escorted by sentimental "pie-in-the-sky." Instead, there should rise up before us the great apophatic antinomy of the cross and the glory, which I mentioned earlier. A God so powerful that he can create other free beings, takes risks and so becomes vulnerable. A God who comes alongside humankind in death and suffering to open up before him unexpected vistas of resurrection; to transform situations of despair -- as Patriarch Athenagoras was wont to say -- into situations of childbirth. A God who does not appear overwhelming and distant, but "hollowed out" by his love; a God who stands forever between us and nothingness. This God basically asks of us a "change of heart," a cry *de profundis*, in order to offer us, in his life-giving Spirit, the royalty of a creative love. For he creates the human being "in his image": like him a "supra-essential secret" revealed in love. So we have, revealed in Christ, God and man, each one both secret and a gift of oneself, both other and not-other ever, more unknown than known, wholly unknowable and wholly communicable, giving a vital sense to the distinction of Gregory Palamas between essence and energies. Above all, finally, are we capable of showing the richness of the trinitarian dogma, concerning a God who is unique but not solitary, who is so much a "super-unity" -- in the words of Denys the Areopagite -- that he bears within himself the breath of the "other"? In Christ, before him, beneath the flames of the Spirit, this trinitarian existentialism communicates itself to humankind. The Christian creed of the person, does it have another origin? This trinitarian approach, that is, the ecclesial approach, to human beings and to inter-human relations, could it not overcome the opposition between the individual and comradeship that bedevils secularized society? Could it not become the lever of history, a forward thrust towards the future, by reconciling the unifying of humanity and the re-affirmed identity of every person and of every culture? In commenting on the luminous apparition of the icon of the Trinity at the end of his film on Andrey Rublev, Tarkovsky writes: "Here at last is the Trinity -- great, serene, filled with a quivering joy out of which human brotherhood pours. The effective division of one into three and the triple union into single unit provide a magnificent prospect for the future still scattered through the centuries...".

c) Transfiguration and divino-humanity

The Russian religious philosophers, whose thought I wish to prolong for they have begun to shed a pentecostal light on the processes of secularization, tried to extend to culture and to society the individual ascetic notion of *transfiguration*. From the angle of an *active eschatology*, it is the effort to enlighten culture and society through the radiance of liturgical and spiritual life reaching out into an inventive love. Here there intervenes, for these thinkers, the theme of *divino-humanity*. Christendom has often taken God's part against the human being's, and the modern world the human being's against God's. But God and the human being are not opposed to one another; they unite and commune in Christ without separation or confusion. Divino-humanity leaves room for the Holy Spirit and for creative freedom. We need this light in order to face the important issues that Christians can no longer avoid at the dawning of the third millenium: the theme of "gnosis," the problem of the body and the earth, the encounter with non-

Christian religions. We have intuition about the paths we shall have to prepare: that of the "conscious heart" -- of heart and mind together -- that of the body undergoing resurrection, beginning to live within the soul, in a liturgy at once traditional and renewed, in an ascetic form of life suited not only to the monk but also to the creative human being and to the married state; the path, too, of a "eucharistic" relationship with the earth, a meditation on nature, on the *logoi* of things -- a symbolic and poetic knowledge, enlightening and orientating a purely rational approach; finally, the path of the integration in Christ, through the Holy Spirit, of the inner world and of transcendance, of me and thee -- that is, of the two "spiritual hemispheres" of humanity which, metaphorically speaking, one could call the Hindu hemisphere and the Semitic hemisphere.

At the same time, the concept of divino-humanity should cast a different light on the conquests and researches of modern humanism. As Patriarch Ignatius IV of Antioch said in his lecture at the Sorbonne, we shall go further than Marx, Nietzsche and Freud. We shall go further than Marx because we know that there are no infrastructures or superstructures, but that all the structures of history react one upon another without any possible synthesis other than the one, beyond conceptualization, of the person rooted at once in the earth and in the heavens. We shall go further than Nietzsche because we have encountered the "dancing God" of the *parecclesion* frescoes at Chôra, in Constantinople: a lightening body leaping to snatch Adam and Eve, you and me, from their tombs and to give back to humankind its vocation of created creator. We shall go further than Freud, because asceticism teaches us to free desire from needs and to "give it back to its origin," as St Gregory Palamas said. It is only when the heart opens up, revealing depths of light long sunk in unconsciousness, that its desire can reach out infinitely into space, into resurrection. If it does not, then its pulsations flow backwards in a death current.

A word in conclusion

In a modern, secularized society, the church -- or rather (in the west) the churches -- have their place, if they can find it. It is not a place of domination. Yet that does not mean that it is a marginal place (a place on the fringe), a ghetto of fear and conceit standing aloof from culture and community life. The church, the churches, have to orientate themselves without fear or conceit so as to come face-to-face with this society, with the certainty that society needs persons of faith in order to exist, for "the church is the heart of the world, even if the world does not heed its heart," to quote Metropolitan George Khodr. This is exactly the situation that the second and third century apologists strove for with regard to the Roman state. This prophetic partnership will sometimes be polemical, sometimes inspirational. It is in itself an aspect of divino-humanity that needs exploring. Does this alloy announce a divino-humanism still unthinkable for us, in the glowing mould of a liberated freedom, of the Middle Ages and of the Renaissance, that of which men like Nicholas Berdiaeff and Maurice Clavel dreamed? I do not know. I know only that twentieth century Christianity -- in particular the Orthodox Church -- has numbered in its ranks a vast host of martyrs, we should not forget the "white martyr" of monks. I know only that, there, there is a nucleus of energy which, if it does not turn aside from contemporary intelligence but rather fertilizes it, is capable of turning the tables of history.

WITNESSING IN A PLURALISTIC SOCIETY

Fr Khajay BARSAMIAN

The present state of the ecumenical movement is of decisive significance for the whole life and work of the Christian churches. No church can stand outside the movement, which leads to and prompts a fresh reconsideration of the whole meaning of the existence and mission of the church.

"Your will be done," is the prayer and the purpose of this Orthodox mission conference. The will of God is the salvation of the world: "For God so loved the world that he gave his only Son, that whoever believes in him should not perish but have eternal life. For God sent the Son into the world, not to condemn the world, but that the world might be saved through him" (John 3:16-17). Christ was sent to bring the world into the life of God. This was the mission of Christ. He transmitted this mission to his disciples and through them to the church, which is Christ's presence in the world. Hence, the mission of the church is based on Christ's mission, namely, to continue the work for the salvation of humanity. Without mission there is no church, because mission belongs to the very nature of the church, whatever the conditions of its life may be.

We are gathered here, as representatives of the Eastern Orthodox and Oriental Orthodox churches, in order to reflect on the nature of Orthodox mission in the contemporary world. My task is to speak about the Oriental experience in general and the Armenian Church in particular in the "American scene."

The difficult task of the Oriental Orthodox churches

First, please allow me to mention that conferences, consultations and meetings of an ecumenical nature have provided opportunities for the Oriental Orthodox churches (i.e. the Armenian Orthodox Church, the Coptic Orthodox Church, the Ethiopian Orthodox Church, the Syrian Orthodox Church, the Syrian Orthodox Church in India) to make their presence felt by their sister churches of east and west, as part of the integral picture of the Christian church in the world today. The contribution of the Oriental Orthodox churches to the ecumenical movement is becoming a significant factor in the ongoing process in which Christian churches all over the world are involved today in their common search for a deeper understanding of their faith and their unity.

On the basis of such experiences, the Oriental Orthodox churches have now entered the new stream of Christian thought that continues today to stir the minds and hearts of men and women in their search for adequate solutions to the manifold and complicated problems of this century.

The Oriental Orthodox churches constitute a group of communities, peoples and nations that, in terms of race, language and culture, display the widest possible diversity. They are present not only in their native countries but are spread throughout the world.

Because of the impact of the ecumenical movement, the unity of these churches was not only revealed as a living reality, but was also increasingly consolidated through contacts, visits and meetings, which culminated in the historic event, the "Conference of the Heads of the Oriental Orthodox Churches" held in Addis Ababa, 15-21 January 1965. For the first time since the fourth and fifth centuries, the heads of these sister churches were seeing and meeting each other in the whole company of the family. Thus they were realizing through personal experience the spiritual strength and firmness that lie in unity, harmony and cooperation carried in the spirit of Christian fellowship.

This conference opened a new era. Its findings and resolutions are embodied in a report, under six chapters:

(a) The modern world and our churches; (b) Cooperation in theological education; (c) Cooperation in evangelism; (d) Our relations with other churches; (e) Instituting machinery for the maintenance of permanent relations among the churches; (f) A statement on peace and justice in the world.

After so many centuries of isolation and estrangement, one could not expect swift and big leaps towards rapprochement and cooperation. It is universally known that these churches were persecuted long and hard by various powers in the world.

The last crisis suffered by some of these churches was the first world war when millions of their faithful were massacred and deported; churches, sanctuaries and monasteries were desecrated and habitations ruined. Soon after the war, however, with the collapse of the Ottoman Empire, they were freed from the heavy yoke and were given more liberal living conditions, particularly in the countries of the Middle East, some west European countries and in the United States and Canada. The past half century has provided these churches with a God-given opportunity for recovery and regeneration, with new aspirations for a more effective and fruitful witness to God and humankind.

This, however, does not mean that the situation is completely free from all obstacles. The growth of the communities of these Oriental Orthodox churches in the western countries marks the beginning of a new destiny. In these countries, which is, generally-speaking, the diaspora, churches have opportunities to recover their spiritual dynamism in the context of comparatively peaceful situations. But there are also difficulties. The western world, in which these churches live today, is not their world, but a world challenging them. We cannot ignore the fact that it is a different world for them, a world that in many ways is alien. There are a myriad of problems confronting modern human beings -- problems pertaining to their faith, their personal selves, their relationships to other people.

One of the major problems of modern civilization is the tendency to conceive of and to live life in purely secular terms. Secularism leads to the imprisonment of the whole human being in what is only part of his/her being. In western thought there is a tendency to draw a dividing line between the church and the secular world. With such a concept, the church is recognized as that milieu where every person can communicate with God, other spheres of human life being understood as independent of God in which humankind can live a life unconscious of God's presence and guidance. The world is one. It is God's world, for it is God's creation. The church does not stand apart from the modern world, but, on the contrary, should be at its very centre. Therefore, the church is to be present in all aspects of human life since its mission is the salvation of the world, which is the will of God.

Thus, the diaspora represents a unique situation for Eastern and Oriental Orthodoxy. Still preserving their national identities and canonical link with their mother churches, still worshipping in the traditional liturgical language, the churches of the Eastern and Oriental Orthodox diaspora must decide whether they are or they are not committed to a real mission in their new environment and, if they are, must tackle the problems of communicating the gospel.

The Armenian Church

I would like to continue by speaking about the mission of the Armenian Orthodox Church in diaspora, and particularly in the United States of America, since there is where my home is. I believe, however, that certain points and considerations that I will present are common to us all.

The diaspora has been a permanent aspect of Armenian life throughout history. Armenians have emigrated almost continuously for one reason or another. Deportation and migration continued throughout the centuries on a larger or smaller scale. But none of the mass deportations equalled the nature, scope and consequences of those that took place between 1915-1922. In fact, during this period almost two million Armenians were massacred by the Turks and the rest were forcefully deported outside their homeland. Following the massacres and deportations of this period, the situation of the Armenian people presented a picture of complete desolation. They had to migrate to wherever they could find refuge: the Middle East, Europe (mainly France), the United States and South America. The first years were a period of settlement and adjustment. They now lived in new countries, they met new people, they began to speak new languages, they adopted new customs, they came into contact with new cultures. Indeed, the recovery and revival of the Armenian Church in the diaspora is amazing. As in the past, the Armenian Church carries on her mission with ever-increasing dedication and renewed vision, even though problems and difficulties exist.

The Armenian Church in the United States

The society of the United States is composed of many nationalities and ethnic backgrounds as a result of the immigration of different peoples. The colourful blending of the multi-communal society into one reflects the diversity of the cultures and uniqueness of its expression. At the same time, there is that other introspective phenomenon in the USA whereby the social, ethnic and cultural factors of diverse characters operate to draw Americans into particular ethnic or religious groups. It is precisely the combination of religion and nationality that constitutes ethnic identification for a considerable number of Americans.

The Armenian community in the United States is perhaps one of the smallest. Like other early arriving immigrant groups, the Armenians underwent every process of naturalization and made themselves part of the formation of the American society. Armenians became very conscious of identifying and locating themselves as Armenians in America, in terms of nationality and religion. As a matter of course, the formation of the American society, influenced by the immigrations, warranted the unmistakable interchange of ethnicity and religion, thus granting perpetual patterns of self-definition and self-recognition in the land of freedom. The difficulties have not shaken the foundations of the Armenian ethnic and religious structure in America.

The following question comes to mind: When did the Armenians begin to come to America? Did the Armenians bring along their own church language, traditions and ethnic culture? Were Armenians able to cling to their religious traditions? What is the nature of the Armenian Church, and what is the impact of that church on its faithful followers in the United States? What are the achievements of the Armenian Church in the mission of the Church of God in America?

In his out-dated and yet dependable book, *The Armenians in America,*[1] Vartan Malcom, an Armenian lawyer, mentioned that the first recorded Armenian arrived in America in 1618 in the Jamestown colony in Virginia. It is assumed that he was invited to Virginia to develop its tobacco plantations.

Various statistics reveal that prior to 1870, the Armenian community of America did not exceed 100, and was formed mainly by students coming from Constantinople. After 1870, dozens of Armenians came to the United States from Turkey. They came as labourers and merchants, their chief intention to earn money and return to their homeland in order to improve the miserable lives of their loved ones. But the continued oppressions and persecutions by the Ottoman Sultans forced many other Armenians to leave their homeland. Therefore, by 1890, Armenians were scattered in various cities of America.

Realizations and challenges

Wherever Armenians went, they looked for an Armenian church, because they identified themselves with that church. As one of the famous poets said, "the Armenian Church is the birthplace of my spirit." Armenians have always understood that the church is the living presence of God in the midst of their lives and history. The Church in Armenia, beyond its institutional manifestations, was, in fact, the re-incarnation of Christian faith in all its features and implications and its full integration into the very texture of the life of the nation.

In the USA the need for the organization of the Armenian Church was first felt in Worcester, Massachusetts. Two hundred and fifty Armenians decided at a meeting to ask the Armenian Patriarch of Constantinople to send a priest. On 25 July 1889, the Very Rev. Hovsep Saradjian arrived in Worcester, and celebrated the first divine liturgy three days later. Consequently, the first Armenian church was built in 1889 in Worcester. In the meantime, the number of Armenians kept growing. By 1897 there were six clergymen serving in different cities. On 16 October 1898, the American Diocese of the Armenian Church was formally established by Catholicos Mkrtich Khrimian. The first clergy conference took place on 17-18 June 1901, and the first Diocesan Assembly, which adopted the Diocesan by-laws, met in Worcester on 12 June 1902.

Gradually churches were built or purchased in various cities. The sister diocese in California was established in 1927 with a separate bishop. In 1957, the Diocese of the Armenian Church of America became a member of the National Council of Churches of Christ in the Unites States. Though the church experienced notable success, there were also periods of crisis. This recurrence of crises is ascribed to a number of factors:

> (a) The Armenian national character with its individualistic and sometimes paranoic aspects; (b) the deep cultural shock experienced as a result of immigration; (c) a pervasive leadership crisis among clergy; (d) the politicization of church and community; (e) the confusion of Armenian national destiny with the church's Christian mission; (f) the jurisdictional conflict; (g) geographical diffuseness of the parishes in the USA; (h) the multiple

waves of migration; (i) the persistence of traditionalism in the Armenian Church.

This critical account of Armenian Church history should not overshadow the achievements and strengths of the Armenian Church in America. It is to be noted that the Armenian Church not only has succeeded in surviving in the "foreign" American environment, but has also registered significant advances.

Comparatively speaking, tremendous strides have been taken during the past three decades in the construction of new churches in various communities in the United States. On 28 April 1968, Vazken I, Supreme Patriarch and Catholicos of all Armenians, consecrated the St Vartan Armenian Cathedral in New York. The culmination of years of planning and effort brought into being an authentic Armenian cathedral and cultural centre that serve as the heart of the diocese. To date, there are about 120 Armenian parishes in the United States, including the Armenian churches under the jurisdiction of the Catholicosate of Antelias, Lebanon.

The leaders of the Armenian Church in the United States continue to carry out the work of the church with the same zeal towards the hopeful future of the mission of the Armenian Church in America. The achievements of the church are many:

(a) a theological school; (b) church youth organizations; (c) a network of Sunday schools; (d) parish schools for Armenian language and culture; (e) choir and church music; (f) liturgical renewal projects; (g) new parish developments; (h) summer Christian education programs; (i) social service programs; (j) training programs for deacons and altar boys; (k) ecumenical relations.

Through the education of Armenian clergymen in the USA in recent years, various new developments have been accomplished. Inspiration is found among many of the pastors of the parishes. Sunday schools, youth movements, social services, greater importance given to Christian education, ecumenical activities -- to mention a few examples -- are the manifestations of the spirit of the mission of the Armenian Church in America.

Looking towards the future

As a result of the continuous arrival of new immigrants to the United States, the Armenian community is constantly growing. For political and economic reasons, Armenians have been landing in the United States from Soviet Armenia, the Middle Eastern countries, Turkey, and some of the Eastern European countries. At present there are approximately 800,000 Armenians living in different parts of the United States. Although the arrival of the new immigrants marks the growth of the Armenian community and Church in America, it also brings crises. There are conflicts between the recent arrivals and those long established in the United States. They all belong to the same nation and the same church, but they come from different social, cultural and political environments.

It is true too that the Armenian Church in America lives in a non-Orthodox world, western in its religious traditions, secular in its culture, and pluralistic in its "world view."

Armenians should be aware of the tremendous spiritual implications and the challenge of the new situation in America. We should not forget the fact that, culturally, the Armenian Church in America is exposed to the western way of life and the western vision and experience of the world. We should never convince ourselves that only by performing the Armenian liturgical services do we preserve the spirit of the Armenian Church.

Armenian history has shown that deep roots of history and religion are the strongest ties that bring people together. But today we find a gap between the church and modern society. The preservation of the identity and distinctive characteristics of the Armenian Church is an absolute principle that cannot be compromised, minimized or overlooked. Particularly in the fluctuating situation of the diaspora, the need to maintain the national character of the church is highly important. Yet there are certain things in the church that need revision and adaptation. The spiritual side of the church's mission cannot receive any impetus or stimulus if the spiritual needs of human beings in this century are not clearly discerned and adequately dealt with. The younger generation that has been born and brought up in America must be cared for in different ways and by different methods.

The Armenian Church has made notable attempts to adjust to American circumstances. It has given up little of its traditional essence, and has preserved its ethnic-national character. The sacred classical language remains the main medium of worship. The sacramental and doctrinal base remains intact. The Armenian Church, however, has not survived as long as it has by accelerated "reform" or acculturation, but by being the national repository of the spiritual values of old Armenia.

"Christian mission to the world"

During the recent pastoral visit of His Holiness Vazken I, Supreme Patriarch and Catholicos of All Armenians, to the United States and Canada, the Patriarch made the following remarks in his address delivered in New York City on 1 November 1987:

> We live in an age in which religious life is, at one level, characterized by the ecumenical concept, the basic proposition of which is the unity of Christian churches and reinforcement of world Christian brotherhood through and in the love of Christ. Our church, the Armenian Church, historically belonging to the great family of ancient Orthodox churches of the east, cannot remain detached from the ecumenical movement. It brings its contribution with witness proper to it, through the theological principles of its fathers and monks, and by its

cooperation towards the solution of religious, moral and social problems facing the modern world....

The younger generation is the future of our church. It is our request to all that you make every effort to see to it that not a single one of your young people is excluded from being a part of the church youth organizations and the Armenian Sunday schools....

For seventeen centuries, the Armenian Church has been a Christian mission to the world. Be proud of your Christian faith, national and spiritual life. Do not falter, do not hesitate, do not waver. Stay firm and unchangeable on the rock of your sacred faith, faithful to the Orthodox theology of our ancestors, faithful to the rules and canons of our church traditions. Live and work united through love, having gathered collectively around you all the faithful people here in the United States.

NOTES

1. Vartan Malcolm, *The Armenians in America*, Boston, 1919 (reprinted San Francisco, 1969).

THEOLOGICAL CONSIDERATIONS

MISSION FOR UNITY OR UNITY FOR MISSION?

- An Ecclesiological / Ecumenical Perspective -

Fr K.M. GEORGE

The new awakening

Very recently, in a prestigious Indian newspaper, there appeared an extended book review by Ram Swarup, a Hindu columnist. The title given to the review article was "Christianity Mainly for Export."[1] The book under review was *Mission Handbook: North American Ministries Overseas*, published by World Vision International, an American evangelical agency with an annual budget of 84 million dollars.[2] The article begins by quoting Mark 16:15-16: "Go into the world and preach the gospel to the whole creation. He who believes and is baptized will be saved; but he who does not believe will be condemned." The writer, who qualifies western missionary work as "soul-saving business," "corporate enterprise," "proselytizing," etc., quotes extensively from the *Handbook* and picks up revealing statistics.

Ram Swarup quotes from the writings of the Texas-based "Gospel for Asia" group: "The Indian sub-continent, with one billion people, is a living example of what happens when Satan rules the entire culture....India is one vast purgatory in which millions of people are literally living a cosmic lie. Could Satan have devised a more perfect system for causing misery?"[3] He has other citations in the same vein. The reader is given a hellish picture of western multi-billion dollar missionary activity. The inevitable conclusion of the reviewer is that "Christianity is losing its hold in Western countries, but they still keep it for export to the third world." Referring to "the powerful missionary lobby" behind the UN Declaration on Human Rights, which states that every individual has the right to embrace the religion or belief of his/her choice, the Hindu writer asks: "But is there to be no similar charter that declares that countries, cultures and peoples of tolerant philosophies and religions who believe in the famous quote 'live and let live' also have a right to protection against aggressive, systematic proselytizing? Are its well-drilled legionaries to have a free field?"[4]

Some of our more enlightened mainline churches, which are engaged in more sophisticated missionary activity, may dispose of it as sectarian fundamentalist rubbish. But to the vast non-Christian populations in many parts of the world it makes no difference. Missionary work is missionary work, that is the aggressively patronizing, culturally-oppressive domination of two-thirds of the world by the powerful western minority wielding the world's wealth and military might, and using the gospel of Christ as a pretext for furthering their political and economic vested interests.

I use this article not simply to show how the multi-million evangelical empires, equipped with the latest electronic media and communication channels, work in our world, but also to point out the new awareness that is being built up in ancient religions of the world, such as Hinduism and Buddhism. The primary components of this revivalist awareness are suspicion of every Christian activity and complete resistance to it. Even Mother Teresa's dedicated work for the poor is being discredited by some of these anti-missionary circles, primarily because some of the western evangelical agencies quote Mother Teresa out of context, highlighting her missionary zeal, and use her work as propaganda material for their proselytizing evangelical business. When resistance to the western missionary initiative began, most of the missionary bodies switched to recruiting and fostering indigenous agencies in the hope that the pill would be swallowed with the indigenous coating. These agencies, however, are heavily and totally funded by their mother bodies, and the "pagans" are intelligent enough to detect all covering and coating. What is at stake is the authenticity of the proclamation of the life-giving gospel.

The fraud, vested interests and big money that accompany the word render it vain and counter-productive.

The awakening of awareness in ancient religions and older civilizations indicated here is different from the awakening of the nations of the east described by Lord Balfour, the first speaker at the Edinburgh Missionary Conference of 1910. Balfour said, in the prevailing mood of optimism created by the imperial expansion, "Nations in the East are awakening. They are looking for two things -- they are looking for enlightenment and for liberty. Christianity alone of all religions meets these demands in the highest degree. There cannot be Christianity without liberty...."[5] Balfour spoke of liberty while his church connived with the British empire to hold millions of people in bondage. The new awakening in the nations of the east rejects the "enlightenment and liberty" offered by the religion of the colonial masters. The way in which Christianity was preached to these nations was a great disservice to the gospel of Christ.

Two assumptions

It is a known fact that the major impetus for the church unity movement came from missionary motivations in the early part of this century. The great missionary motto, "evangelization of the world in this generation," was launched by John R. Mott in 1910. The urgency of bringing the gospel to the unsaved millions impelled the various Protestant denominations to come together and seek a common ground and common strategy for missionary action. It was a very practical and empirical search. It was expected that unity begin in the mission field, and devising a common overseas missionary strategy would perhaps bring in "a greater measure of unity in ecclesiastical matters at home," and "increased hope of international peace among the nations of the world" (Lord Balfour). There were two assumptions behind this search for unity:

(a) Although speakers at the Edinburgh conference, such as Archbishop Davidson of Canterbury, expressed the idea that "the place of missions in the life of the church must be the central place and none other," it was generally assumed that unity of the churches would be instrumental in the effective carrying out of the all-important missionary task. The same idea of the instrumental character of church unity for world evangelization, and through that for world peace, was prominently held during many subsequent years. The Tambaram (Madras) Conference in 1938, the 50th anniversary of which was recently celebrated, affirmed that "world peace will never be achieved without world evangelization," and thus urged the churches "to *unite* in the supreme work of world evangelization until the kingdoms of this world become the Kingdom of our Lord." Thus, the predominant thrust of the period before the formation of the World Council of Churches (WCC), was unity *for* mission. The emphasis was not on the church, nor on the unity of the church, but on the evangelistic mission, the outgoing, converting civil gatherings, and number-increasing mission. There was no real search in missionary circles for ecclesiological grounds for unity as it appears later, for instance, in the Faith and Order movement, which expressed the need "to penetrate behind our divisions to a deeper and richer understanding of the mystery of the God-given union of Christ with His church" (Lund, 1952). Theologically speaking, the "unity for mission" call assumed that mission was different from unity. It could not go beyond the notion of the practical coming together of various Protestant denominations for strengthening work in the mission field. Division was detrimental to mission and therefore had to be rectified. Unity was the means by which mission could be accomplished.

(b) Churches and missionary bodies in the pre-WCC period, which coincided with the colonial-imperial period, apparently assumed that concern for unity and mission was an exclusively Christian concern. Perhaps they did not openly acknowledge that the mission that they conceived was modelled on another complex and universal political mission of the imperial rulers. The gigantic movement of colonial expansion, which spanned several centuries, attempted to accomplish a certain unity by bringing various peoples, cultures and continents under the authority of western imperial powers. It was an invading, conquering and colonizing mission. In spite of its openly lustful search for wealth and power, the prophets of that mission identified it with a divine calling. It was "the white man's burden," as the poet Rudyard Kipling, one of the staunchest advocates of imperialism, conceived it. He was convinced that "the responsibility for governing India had been placed by the *inscrutable decree of providence* upon the shoulders of the British race."

Mission in humankind's way

Vasco de Gama, the Portuguese explorer, landed in Kerala, India, in 1498 where a Christian church had already taken root from the Apostolic era. It is reported that in answer to a question posed by an Indian, "what were the Portuguese looking for in Asia?" he said: "Christians and spices." And his landing on the Malabar coast marked the beginning of a conquering and proselytizing mission by Portuguese Roman Catholics, and later, by British missionaries, inflicting deep wounds on the already existing Christian community in India. The Portuguese *conquistadores* defined their motive for embarking on this mission as "to serve God and His Majesty, to give light to those who are in the darkness and to grow rich as all men desire to do."[6]

Therefore, what the west European churches conceived as their unique mission of saving the pagans and gathering them for the patriarchal embrace of western Christendom was mainly an extension of the great commercial and political mission already universally launched by the colonial-imperial powers. "Mission," whether in the political, commercial or religious sense, was essentially a state enterprise. "Religion supplied the pretext and gold the motive. The technological progress accomplished by Atlantic Europe during the fourteenth and fifteenth centuries provided the means."[7] Rarely did any European engaged in this mission distinguish the mission of Christ from that in His Majesty's service. The tragedy of mission in the post-colonial imperial period is that the basic attitudes and methods of the imperial mission still lingered. The division of the world into those who are saved and those unsaved, or yet to be saved, remains in Christian missionary attitudes and in political-economic categories like the new three-tier universe of first, second and third worlds.

These two assumptions of the past western missionary enterprise are mentioned in order to suggest that we have to go far beyond them in order to enter into a new understanding of the nature of unity and the mission of the church. On the one hand, we need to transcend the alternatives -- unity for mission or mission for unity. The understanding of the church as the body of Christ, manifesting the kingdom in unity, holiness, catholicity and apostolicity, is central to us. Unity and mission are integral to this. On the other hand, our mission is not on behalf of the powers of this world, but on behalf of the one whose "kingdom is not of this world" (John 18:36). God's mission has to be weaned from its past political, imperialistic matrix. This is the dialect of Christ's mission today -- the historical visible, tangible dimension of the life of the church expressing itself in concrete situations and moments on the one hand, and, on the other, the transcendent, ineffable, eschatological experience of the body of Christ, the Lord whose kingdom permeates the whole creation, both visible and invisible.

Manifesting the kingdom

Manifesting God's rule or kingdom is the mission *par excellence* of the church. We know that the fullness of the kingdom cannot be identified with anything within the created realm. It is a kingdom ever present and ever coming. God's rule is inexhaustible and is identified only with the incomprehensible nature of the Triune God. However, created reality is thoroughly permeated with the power of the kingdom. Everything that *is*, visible or invisible, is under God's rule. The church, as the community of the Holy Spirit, is called to make this power manifest in our world, to witness where it is descernibly present, whether in cultures, religions or secular ideologies; to discern it where it is confused with the powers of this world; to proclaim it, especially to the poor and the victims of injustice, as "the Lord's year of grace" for liberation.

The presence of the church as the icon of the kingdom is mission in the deepest sense. Just as Christ was fulfilling his mission by his incarnate presence in the world, the church's iconic presence in itself constitutes the mission. In the physical presence of the Lord the reality of God and the destiny of creation were together manifested. We understand the presence of the church as a continuous *parousia*, enabling us to participate in the mission of Christ. This understanding of the church, of course, does not conform to the notion of the church as an instrument -- an instrument for mission, for social transformation, for uniting the nations of the world. The instrumentalist language tends to treat Christ, church, unity, mission and world as unrelated realities that somehow must be linked with each other. But in the biblical and patristic understanding of the church as the body of Christ and the icon of the kingdom manifesting the glory of God and illuminating the future of creation, the integral unity of Christ, church and the creation is presupposed as fundamental. Mission in our times is to rediscover this unity from within and not to impose unity from a detached alien and superior perspective, as was done in colonial, imperial times, and as it is being done in our neo-colonial times.

Prof. Nikos Nissiotis classifies all ecclesiological trends in contemporary systematic theology mainly in two categories -- the pro-catholicizing and the pro-congregationalist.[8] The first is conceived on the basis of incorporation of all in Christ and sharing the same experience in the sacramental body, and implies an inseparable single communion. The second ecclesiological category starts with the gathering of the people of God by God's word. The community "hears" and acknowledges the supremacy of the word of God and shares in the prophetic actualization of the evangelical messages in the world. Although these two trends are integral dimensions of an authentic ecclesiology, our loyalties are often in conflict and we attach ourselves to either one or the other in a mutually inclusive way.

Perhaps the different historical experiences of the western and eastern churches encouraged the deepening of the separation between these two ecclesiological trends. The churches that live under hostile regimes would perhaps show an inclination to the first, and the churches that live in political and economic systems that emphasize geographical outreach as the essence of growth would be inclined towards the latter. In our understanding of the church as the iconic manifestation of the kingdom, these two ecclesiological dimensions are taken together as two sides of the same coin. I would like to indicate some of the major aspects, as they appear to me, of the church's life as manifesting the kingdom in relation to unity and mission.

In the sayings of the Desert Fathers, we often see young monks, who are tormented by disturbing thoughts and flights of fantasy, approach the elders for advice. The usual advice is "stay in your cell." The risen Lord told the disciples: "Stay in the city until you are clothed with power from on high" (Luke 24:49) before they went out to announce the good news. The church's staying in the city of Jerusalem in prayer and waiting for the Holy Spirit was an exercise in unity. The eucharistic community that worships and gives thanks to the Lord in the "cell" of prayer on behalf of all creation continues that act of gathering the whole order of creation to be offered to God. The church joins the high-priestly prayer of our Lord "that they all may be one."

In the Orthodox tradition, the predominant image is that of the saint and not of the outgoing preacher-missionary. The saint prays and receives the creation of God with hospitality. The missionary preaches and offers, often aggressively, in order to give. I am not drawing a mutually exclusive contrast between the saint and the missionary. There are missionaries who are saints, and saints in the Orthodox tradition who were missionaries. The world, however, is healed and transfigured more by the praying saint than by the thundering preachers. It is the saint who, manifesting God's tender love and receiving all creatures in divine hospitality, is genuinely sensitive to the riches of other religions, to different cultures, to "all sentient beings." The crusading missionary is afire with the message he proclaims, but can be totally lacking in receptivity and sensitivity. Perhaps this is a stereotyped image of the past. Today we need to combine in our experience of our church the true saint and the genuine missionary whose sole concern is manifesting the kingdom and not annexing new territories.

Division and conflict in our world are mainly the work of the political powers allied with economic interests. The military-industrial complex of demonic dimensions will continue to strike at the root of harmony and unity among peoples of the world. Disunity is essential for the survival of those forces of evil. The churches in many parts of the world are unknowingly drawn to be instruments of these powers. At the same time, there are strong movements in various churches that stand up prophetically against the powers that break God's word and sow enmity among the people. This should challenge the Orthodox churches to witness to the kingdom in the true sense of *martyria.* How could we keep ourselves away from identifying God's will for the world with the political will and economic designs of dominant powers? This is a major question which we must answer when concerning ourselves with the mission of the church.

The mission of the church is an act of *epiclesis,* calling the Holy Spirit to descend upon the whole creation. It constitutes an act of creative unification. The priestly gesture at the moment of *epiclesis* in the Syrian Orthodox liturgy is especially significant. In the fluttering and cyclic movements symbolizing the Spirit, the priest invokes the Spirit to hover over the elements and to dwell within the Holy Eucharist, thus to infuse into the whole created reality. If the church's historical existence can become an act of *epiclesis*, calling upon the Spirit to descend and dwell within our world, to transfigure it, then the church's mission is accomplished. The Spirit also liberates us from our barrenness of thought and attitude and makes us aware of the truth that mission in Christ's way has many faces and many ways, not only one. St Paul, writing to the Thessalonians, said, "For our Gospel came to you not only in word, but also in power and in the Holy Spirit and with full conviction (I Thess. 1:15). This is the way in which the gospel must be proclaimed in our world too.

NOTES

1. Ram Swarup, "Christianity Mainly for Export," in: *Times of India*, March 14, 1988.

2. Samuel Wilson and John Siewert (eds.), *Mission Handbook: North American Ministries Overseas*, California: MARC, a Division of World Vision International, 1986.

3. Swarup, *op. cit.*

4. *Ibid.*

5. "History and Records of the Edinburgh Conference," p. 145, quoted in Philip Potter, "From Edinburgh to Melbourne," in *Your Kingdom Come*, Geneva: World Council of Churches, 1980, p. 10.

6. Carlo M. Cipolla, *European Culture and Overseas Expansion*, Penguin Books, 1970, p. 99.

7. Carlo M. Cipolla, *op. cit.*, p. 101.

8. Nikos Nissiotis, "The Church as a Sacramental Vision and the Challenge of Christian Witness," in G. Limouris (ed.), *Church, Kingdom, World*, Geneva: World Council of Churches, 1986, Geneva, p. 100 ff.

THE EUCHARIST AS MISSIONARY EVENT IN A SUFFERING WORLD

Fr Emmanuel CLAPSIS

As Christians, we have freely consented and invited God to reign in history, to change the world, looking forward to the moment when "God will be all in all" (I Cor. 15:28). This is reflected in the Lord's prayer: "Thy kingdom come, thy will be done, on earth as it is in heaven." In Jesus Christ the will of God has been done on earth as it is in heaven (John 4:34; Matt. 26:39,42; Mark 14:36; John 6:38-48). Those who constitute his resurrected body in history, to the extent that they identify with him by the power of the Holy Spirit and therefore doing the will of God, manifest and actualize the good news of salvation to all people. Salvation in this context is understood as a communion of loving obedience and life with God, since life apart from him has been experienced as death. The Christian church proclaims that the only option and hope of life that the world has is derived from the already actualized and coming reality of God's kingdom in which all people, through their identification with Jesus Christ by the power of the Holy Spirit, partake in God's trinitarian life and thus live in his love, peace, joy and justice (Psalm 85:7-13; Isa. 32:17-18; 65:17-25; Rev. 21:1-2).

The Christian message is *"evangelion"* -- good news -- for the whole world that groans for redemption. The good news needs to be consciously known and shared by all who seek liberation from the forces of evil and death. For this reason, Jesus Christ explicitly exhorted his disciples: "Go therefore and make disciples of all nations..." and simultaneously he assured them "... and lo, I am with you always to the close of the age" (Matt. 28-19). The wisdom and the power of their missionary endeavour was given to them by the Holy Spirit (Acts 1:8).

The mission of Jesus' disciples to the world is not theirs, but his, since God does not delegate his salvific mission, but they participate in it by virtue of their identification and communion with him. From this perspective, conversion to Christ is not just a matter of espousing a new set of beliefs or executing new forms of worship; it rather implies a new way of relating to God that decisively affects, to the extent of an ontological change, the totality of our human existence, with significant consequences for the mode and the nature of our relationships with other people and the world at large.

Mission and worship

In addition to his missionary exhortation, Jesus Christ asks his disciples to "gather in my name" (Matt. 18:20) "for the breaking of bread" (Acts 20:7; cf. I Cor. 11:33). In this *synaxis* the early Christians experienced that which is promised for the *Parousia*, namely the eschatological unity of all in Christ: "Just as this loaf was scattered all over the mountains and having been brought together was made one, so let your church be gathered from the ends of the earth in your kingdom."[1] Thus the life of the early Christian community has been shaped by a two-fold orientation: towards the world in a movement of *diastole*, and towards God in that of *systole*. These two orientations constitute the being of the church as mission and liturgy, and neither of these two aspects of the church's being should be confused or separated from the other.[2] This must be further emphasized since in contemporary Christian theology -- with few exceptions -- worship and mission are treated as two totally distinct objects of theological investigation; they are placed in isolated compartments without the possibility of cross-fertilization and without the question of their unity being raised at all. Disunity between worship and mission is contrary to the experience of the apostolic church. In the scriptures the life of Jesus is simultaneously described in terms of both mission and worship. He is "Apostle and High Priest" (Heb. 3:1). In addition, cultic language has been used in order to describe the nature of charity in God's sight: "an odour of a sweet smell, a sacrifice acceptable, well-pleasing to God" (Phil. 4:18; cf. Jas. 1:27).[3]

The unity between mission and worship as inseparable aspects of God's relation to humankind must be affirmed by the Christian church since where disunity prevails, distortion inevitably arises. An exclusive emphasis on cultic life leads to introversion and liturgical escapism from the challenges of history. This was a reality when Amos explicitly condemned worship detached from an active concern for justice (5:21-15). In the same manner Isaiah stated:

> I am disgusted with the smell of incense you burn
> Your Sabbaths, and your religious gatherings.
> They are all corrupted by your sins.
> Yes, stop doing evil
> and learn to do right.
> See that justice is done
> Help those who are oppressed
> Give orphans their rights
> and defend widows (Isa. 1:13ff; cf. Isa. 58:3ff; Jer. 7:2-12, 21-23).

This prophetic tradition was continued in the ministry of Jesus. He referred explicitly to it in one of his discourses with the Pharisees. He appealed to them:

> Go and learn what this means.
> I desire mercy, and not sacrifice (Matt. 9:13; cf. Hos. 6:6).

On another occasion Jesus instructed his disciples that:

> If you are offering your gift at the altar
> and there remember that your brother has something against you,
> leave your gift,
> first be reconciled,
> and then offer your gift (Matt. 5:23-24).

Biblical tradition confirms as an indisputable fact that there is an indissoluble link between worship and service to others, especially the poor. Whenever this reality has weakened in the life of the church, the prophetic voices, like the voice of St John Chrysostom, will remind us:

> Do you want to honour Christ's body? Then do not honour him here in the church with silken garments while neglecting him outside where he is cold and naked.... Of what use is it to weight down Christ's table with golden cups when he himself is dying of hunger? First fill him when he is hungry; then use the means you have left to adorn his table.[4]

The same venerable father of our church states boldly that love for the poor is a liturgy whose altar is more venerable than the one on which the eucharist is celebrated, "the latter being precious by reason of the body of Christ which is received (from it), the other because it is the body of Christ."[5] The point is clear that worship, "the sacrament of the altar," is inconceivable apart from the "sacrament of the poor."[6] They are two facets of one and the same reality of God's active presence in history. Jesus described his mission in terms of: "Bringing good news to the poor, proclaiming release to the captives, recovery of sight to the blind, setting free those who are oppressed" (Luke 4:18).

In the eucharist, the faithful become the living expression of Jesus Christ and therefore participate in his saving mission in the world. They are sent out on mission that includes the liberation of humanity by putting into motion the construction of that new world for which Christ gave his life in love. This means that we can no longer celebrate the eucharist with eyes closed to the needs of the poor and downtrodden.[7] Commitment to Christ in the eucharist carries with it a commitment through Christ to the poor of this world. In this way an indissoluble relationship exists between the celebration of the eucharist and the creation of a better world. Consequently this implies that action for justice constitutes an integral element of the church's mission in the world. Therefore, it is a false dilemma to debate whether the eucharist has priority over social concerns and actions, or vice versa. It should rather be emphasized that they cannot be conceived apart from each other without erroneous consequences for the authenticity of the Christian ethos.

Liturgy without social concern is reduced to ritualism and leads to introversion. It is equally true that *mission* apart from worship reduces Christianity to a religious ideology either of the left or of the right. It becomes a subject of human pride and self-will and it may not serve Christ, but its proprietor. Worship as a communal and God-centred event would help mission to recover its true nature as participation in God's mission. More specifically, the eucharist is the unique liturgical act that brings together in a creative but disturbing unity the vertical and horizontal dimensions of Christian mission and living.

Eucharist and mission

Having defined mission and worship as two distinct but inseparable facets of God's presence and action in the world, we have affirmed their inclusive interdependence and rejected any attempt to subsume either one under the other. The church, through mission, makes the people consciously aware of God's salvific presence and action in the world, and invites them to partake in a new life of communion with the Trinity that decisively shapes their identity as this develops through and in relation to God and other people. This kind of new life is sacramentally actualized and communally experienced in the eucharist, which is the great mystery of our participation in the life of the Holy Trinity, the recapitulation of the entire history of salvation in Christ and the foretaste of the kingdom of God.[8] In it, the faithful, by the invocation of the Holy Spirit, become the body of Christ, in which all respect one another for their unique gifts that the Holy Spirit has bestowed upon them for the building-up of their unity, which is grounded in their baptism: "In one Spirit we were all baptized into one body" (I

Cor. 12:13). In Christ all discrimination among Christians on grounds of history, culture, social status, or sex have been removed (Gal. 3:27f; cf. I Cor. 12:13; Col. 3:11, Eph. 6:8; Jas. 2:2-7). The gift of life in the one body is a call to mutual forgiveness, love and peace (Col. 3:12-15).[9]

Because the Father's purpose for humanity is all-embracing, to the Christian the stranger in need and even the enemy are potentially brothers and sisters.[10] From this perspective, the eucharistic community is a catholic community in the sense that it transcends not only social but also natural divisions, just as will happen in the kingdom of God, of which this community is a revelation and real sign.[11] The light of the eucharistic liturgy projected upon life unmasks as inhuman and false any life reduced to an excessive and egoistic accumulation of material goods, oblivious to the needs of the neighbour, and any mentality of consumption without the joy of sharing. The eucharistic vision is also a judgement on any oppression of the neighbour, since justice, peace, love and service to the neighbour are the only basis for true relations among people and nations.[12]

An encounter with this high eucharistic theology immediately raises questions whether it is possible to discern this kind of communal life in the life of the historical church.[13] We must admit that this eucharistic experience to a great degree has ceased to affect and guide the ecclesiastical consciousness as well as the "world view" of the Christian community.[14] This signifies that in the lives of the believers an undesirable separation between the sacred and the secular has been developed that seriously challenges the sincerity and effectiveness of their worship. Regardless of how we explain this phenomenon theologically, we must insist that in so far as the liturgy fails to produce appropriate fruits in the lives of its participants, the failure is due to a lack or refusal on the human side to encounter God.

The unity of a person with God in the eucharist is actualized when the person is open and receptive to God's grace. It means something more than just not putting an obstacle to it; it calls for the active engagement of the person in its reception (*synergeia*).[15] In this context it is also important to emphasize that unworthy participation in the Lord's supper is, in fact, counter-productive to one's salvation (I Cor. 11:17-34), and it becomes a serious obstacle to the church's mission as much as this is dependent on the life and the witness of those human beings who profess to be church members.

What the faithful become in and through the eucharist is primarily an event by which God, through the operation of the Holy Spirit, unites his people with the risen Lord. Thus, the people of God experience sacramentally in history their eschatological existence as it will be in God's kingdom. However, although this is an immediate experience for them through the celebration of the eucharist, it does not become history since it is an act of God reserved for the *eschata* (meta-history). For this reason, the fathers understood the eucharist not only as a sacramental assembly of what we have already become in the risen Christ but also as a movement, a progress toward this realization.[16] This *kinesis* makes the eucharist a dynamic event of life that shapes the life of its participants who have encountered God as a movement from death to life, from injustice to justice, from violence to peace, from hatred to love, from vengeance to forgiveness, from selfishness to sharing and from division to unity. It has the power to give confidence in the midst of ambiguity, openness in the face of uncertainty and hopeful courage even in the face of death. It has the power to raise people to a new threshold from which they can view reality with new eyes, new hope, new resistance.[17] "One can even say that the Eucharist is, as it were, a transcendent support for all social activity when the latter is directed towards the qualitative unity of all mankind."[18]

This constitutes the church's mission, revealing what we have already become in the risen Christ, and what we will fully experience in his kingdom. Thus Christians, as it becomes evident in the eucharist, draw the being of their identity not from the values of this world but from the being of God and from that which we will be at the end of this age.[19] Baptized Christians, therefore, in the eucharist become a community of people who together unite prayer with action, praise with justice, adoration with transformation, and contemplation with social involvement. As they disperse in history for the proclamation of the Christian gospel, their missionary task is affected not only by their words but also by what they do and how they relate to each other in the context of our fragmented world. Consequently, an essential aspect of the church's mission is realized by the nature of the community that Christians become and are in the process of becoming, through the celebration of the eucharist, which is the springboard and the goal of mission.[20] This, however, presupposes the adoption of an effective process of "consciousness-raising," by which the faithful will be helped to recognize the social implications of what they become in the liturgy, which is not unrelated to what they do outside the church building.

Caution must be exercized here against any kind of reductionism of the utilitarian nature that reduces the eucharist simply to a "useful" event that sanctifies our political agenda and actions. This is usually preceded by an unbalanced theology that maximizes God's immanence while it minimizes or ignores his transcendence. From this perspective, the Christian gospel becomes only an immanent reality or force of social transformation. The eucharist, being an intrinsically eschatological event of theandric origin and nature, invites its participants to experience, understand and criticize life from their unity with God and the coming reign of his kingdom. This perception unmasks the inhumanities and the basic deficiencies of all ideologies by insisting that it is primarily God who changes the world and those who confess his name participate in that process of change by doing his will.[21] Thus, in the eucharist, the faithful celebrate what they have already become in Christ and what the world will become when God's will is done on earth as it is in heaven. This experience determines the witness of the church to the world.

NOTES

1. *Didache*, 9:4 cf. 10,5.

2. Nikos A. Nissiotis, "The Church as a Sacramental Vision and the Challenge of Christian Witness," in *Church Kingdom World -- The Church As Mystery and Prophetic Sign*, Gennadios Limouris, ed., Geneva, 1986, p. 103.

3. J.G. Davies, *Worship and Mission*, London, 1966; Johannes Hofinger, *Worship: The Life of the Missions*, Notre Dame, 1958; idem.,ed., *Liturgy and the Missions*, New York, 1960; Alexander Schememann, *The Eucharist*, New York, 1988; Ion Bria, ed., *Martyria and Mission, The Witness of the Orthodox Churches Today*, Geneva, 1980; idem., ed., *Go Forth in Peace, Orthodox Perspectives on Mission*, Geneva, 1986; George Patronos, *Biblikes proypotheseis tes hierapostoles*, Athens, 1983.

4. John Chrysostom, Homily 50, Mat. Ev. 3-4, in: *MPG*, 58, 508ff.

5. S. Lyonnet, "La nature du culte dans le Nouveau Testament," in J.P. Jossua and Y. Congar, eds., *La Liturgie après Vatican II*, Paris, 1967, p. 383; N.E. Mitsopoulou, *Physis kai latreytikos charakter tôn agathôn ergôn*, Athens, 1969.

6. Olivier Clément, "The Sacrament of the Brother/the Sister," in J.P. Ramalho, ed., *Signs of Hope and Justice*, Geneva, 1980, p. 24.

7. Christians must remember that the Christ who is really, truly and substantially present in the eucharist is the same Christ who is also personally present in the poor and downtrodden of this world. These two presences of Christ must be kept together and understood as complementing each other. We cannot consistently choose the comfortable real presence of Christ in the eucharist and ignore the disturbing personal presence of Christ in the poor and downtrodden.

8. *Report of the New Valamo Consultation*, Geneva, 1978, p. 17.

9. J.C. Haughey, "Eucharist at Corinth: You are the Christ," in *Above Every Name: The Lordship of Christ and Social Systems*, T.E. Clarke, ed., New York, 1980, pp. 107-133.

10. For the ethical presuppositions and consequences of the liturgy, see: Geoffrey Wainwright, *Doxology: A Systematic Theology*, London, 1980, pp. 399-434.

11. John D. Zizioulas, "Eucharist and Catholicity," in his book *Being As Communion*, New York, 1985, pp. 143-169.

12. Dan-Ilie Ciobotea, "The Role of the Liturgy in Orthodox Theological Education," *St. Vladimir's Theological Quarterly*, 31/2, 1985, p. 114.

13. This question was immediately raised whenever Orthodox theologians expressed this kind of theology. (See the discussion and the reaction of the Orthodox Ecclesiological statement of the Valamo Consultation, especially the reactions of José Miguez Bonino on the *Report of the New Valamo Consultation*, Geneva, 1978, pp. 33-36).

14. This problem was articulated by Alexander Schmemann in his article, "Theology and Liturgy," *Greek Orthodox Theological Review*, 17/1, 1972, pp. 86-100.

15. Geoffrey Wainwright, *Doxology*, p. 403; Gennadios Limouris, "The Eucharist as the Sacrament of Sharing: An Orthodox Point of View," *Ecumenical Review*, 38, 1986, p. 401.

16. "Where a people is being harshly oppressed, the Eucharist speaks of the exodus or deliverance from bondage. Where Christians are rejected or imprisoned for their faith, the bread and the wine become the life of the Lord who was rejected by men but has become 'the chief stone of the corner.' Where the church sees a diminishing membership and its budgets are depressing, the Eucharist declares that there are no limits to God's giving and no end to hope in him. Where discrimination by race, sex or class is a danger for the community, the Eucharist enables people of all sorts to partake of the one food and to be made one people. Where people are affluent and at ease with life, the Eucharist says, 'As Christ shares his life, share what you have with the hungry.' Where a congregation is isolated by politics or war or geography, the Eucharist unites us with all God's people in all places and all ages. Where a sister or brother is near death, the Eucharist becomes a doorway into the kingdom of our loving Father," in *Your Kingdom Come -- Report on the World Conference on Mission and Evangelism 1980*, Geneva, 1980, p. 206.

17. On the eschatological nature of the eucharist, see the excellent book by Geoffrey Wainwright, *Eucharist and Eschatology*, London, 1971.

18. G. Limouris, *op. cit.* p. 404.

19. J. Zizioulas, *op. cit.* p. 61.

20. I. Bria, "Liturgy after Liturgy," *Martyria and Mission*, p. 69.

21. On the complexities of the political involvement, see Nikos A. Nissiotis, *Apologia tes elpidas*, Athens, 1975; Emmanuel Clapsis, *Church and Politics*, (an unpublished paper).

ORTHODOX
MISSION
PERSPECTIVES

YOUTH IN MISSION
- Syndesmos' Aspirations in Mission -

Fr Kwame J.A. LABI

The subject of mission in the Orthodox Church, when it comes up in any Orthodox gathering in which I participate, or in any gathering that the Orthodox participate in, makes me a little self-conscious:

1) because it is as if it is the only thing that I ever talk about or wish to talk about -- the only subject that I always manage to come back to, whatever the subject of discussion;

2) it is as if I were, as in a trial, a public trial, one of the chief exhibits.

This, however, is because in September 1982, under the sign of the life-giving Cross (precisely between September 14 and 19) Orthodoxy found yet another convert in Africa. The once independent, purely indigenous African group which called itself the "Orthodox Catholic Church," but which was not canonically Orthodox, became the canonical "Orthodox Church, Ghana" under the Patriarchate of Alexandria. Significantly, this historic event gave the first real substance of this patriarchate's long established Archdiocese of Accra and All West Africa (established or re-established since the 1950s); an Archdiocese that had hitherto served no real African church.

In effect, a new Orthodox church was born, or better still, an old daughter was reborn, an old church renewed (made new); for this was indeed true of our church: An entire community, fifty years old, was (re)baptized and chrismated, and invested with a new order; a set of old priests were (re)taught and (re)ordained to become the first new priests of the new church. In the water of baptism the old indeed died and were resurrected as the new, and were endowed with the new life of the Holy Spirit in the oil of chrismation, as indeed on Pentecost.

I was one of the Lord's humble instruments in this process. As to the circumstances of our church's entrance into Orthodoxy, they were particularly significant: the fifty odd years of our "old" life before the new; the Feast of the Universal Exaltation of the Cross; the very miracle of the discovery of Orthodoxy by our community, leading to my own education at St Vladimir's Orthodox Theological Seminary in New York, etc.. So I have often wondered what the true significance of this event was: what is the purpose of the Orthodox Church in Ghana and in Africa as a whole? What is its role?

Closely related to this event was another process that has played a significant role in giving meaning to the first event. It is the process of our church's involvement with "Syndesmos." In 1980, two years before our community became Orthodox, during the "Syndesmos" youth festival and General Assembly in Valamo, Finland, the youth organization of our church (the Orthodox Youth Organization, Ghana) became a part of the "Syndesmos" process.

I mention this fact not only because I represent "Syndesmos" here (I will talk about "Syndesmos" shortly, and its role and aspirations in mission) but also because indeed in my involvement with "Syndesmos" since 1980, it is in the humble "Syndesmos" involvement in mission that I have found some kind of answer to the questions that the 1982 event in Ghana posed for me. And now let me talk about "Syndesmos." "Syndesmos," for those who do not know, is the "World Fellowship of Orthodox Youth." This does not define it and I am going to try to explain it by telling what it is not.

1) "Syndesmos" is first and foremost, and this is very important for us, *not* a para-ecclesial organization. It is in this

sense an organization that seeks to work and works only within the context of the church.

2) "Syndesmos" is not even a movement. Technically and in practice it is a federation of movements, organizations, associations of youth within the local churches; movements, associations, etc., that are recognized and whose activities are blessed by the local hierarchy. Applications for membership can be considered only if they are endorsed by the hierarchy of the applicants. It is *not* a rebel organization nor an organization for rebel groups. Movements would lose their membership once "Syndesmos" was aware that recognition for that movement had been withdrawn by the local hierarchy.

We cannot here trace the history of "Syndesmos" involvement in mission since its beginnings in the 1950s. But, by way of a quick enumeration, I can mention for instance:

- the Kenyan Youth Project -- in which "Syndesmos" raised some money to sponsor a full-time youth director for the church in Kenya for six years;
- the first Ghana Project of 1982 -- in which "Syndesmos" sent two youth workers from Finland to work with the youth and the church in Ghana for three weeks;
- the second Ghana Project of 1985 -- in which "Syndesmos" sent two youth workers from the United States to work in Ghana with youth leaders, catechists, priests and lay people for a total of ten weeks;
- the theme of the 1980-83 triannium for "Syndesmos" was significantly "Unity and Mission;" it nearly was "Unity *in* Mission." A few papers have been produced on the subject, and a number of well-meaning projects have also been proposed, although the possibilities for bringing them to fruition have not yet been realized.

In these ventures and efforts, the aspirations of the youth of our church, the Orthodox Church throughout the world, have come out clearly:

- The young people of the church today are saying that the missionary fervor of our church has been suffering for too long. It is time for the church to wake up to its responsibilities -- true responsibilities in mission.
- The young people of the church today are saying that too much time is spent talking about mission and too little doing or participating in mission.
- The young people of the church today are saying that too much time is spent glorifying the past, the work and achievements of Sts Cyril and Methodius, and too little in following their footsteps and those who sent them.
- The young people of the church today are saying: we are not merely the object of mission; we are capable of doing mission; we would like to be listened to; we would like to offer our services; we would like to be a part of the process, but an active process.
- The young people of the church today are demanding that the church -- the Orthodox Church, at least -- *unite!* Yes, the division of Christendom is bad enough, but the disunity -- the practical disunity -- of the Orthodox Church is unpardonable. When it comes to our not being able to co-operate even for mission, all aspects of it, we do not know what to say.
- The young people of the church today are saying: we can no longer continue to justify our inactivity by hiding behind refined theological definitions of what Orthodox mission is.
- The young people of the church today are saying: let us renew our church and bring it back to life.
- The young people of the church today are saying: let us begin to die that the church might live.

When I think of my own experiences the same concerns come up.

I have often viewed my role in mission and the role of the youth of my church in Ghana in the light of the 1982 event of my church's entrance into Orthodoxy. And the question is what this event means in terms of Orthodox mission in Africa

-- I am talking about *the* Africa that, as His Grace Bishop Anastasios put it, has for so long been wrong by being deprived of, and I dare use the expression "the true faith."

I come to a sensitive point here: Christianity in my part of Africa did not start with the Orthodox Church. We are one of the latest entrants. Christianity was already firmly established with flourishing churches of the mainline western confessions, of the mainline pentecostal movement and of the "spiritual" pentecostal movement that is mainly represented in the typically African "independent" churches. We entered in the context of an already established Christian pluralism, but one that was and is characterized by -- should I say -- confusion? Should I say unanswered questions -- a question mark hanging over the very approprietness of Christianity as *the* religion for Africa?

What do we, as Orthodox, have to contribute? What is our answer? Are we yet another addition to the proliferation, to the confusion? Or is our church the new prophetic voice that wakens, "the still small voice" that calms the pandemonium and ushers in the real presence of the Lord?

It is when I think of these questions that the concerns that I have expressed earlier acquire a profound significance and a certain urgency for me and my people. We question and challenge certain basic attitudes to mission of Orthodox peoples in much more fortunate and favourable situations.

- We question and challenge the luke-warm attitudes.
- We question and challenge the inactivity, the nominations.
- We question and challenge the triumphalism even where nothing exists.
- We question, we challenge the lack of support, the lack of trust.

We in Africa challenge the church to start doing mission. We challenge *this assembly*, this consultation not only to come up with beautiful papers on our contribution to the "ongoing debate," but also to devise a concrete program of helping the struggling Orthodox churches in Africa, Asia and Latin America.

We talk about the eucharist and the sacrament as being the centre of the church's mission. How are we helping young churches in Africa, for instance, to acquire and lead a normal liturgical life -- something that most of us here take for granted?

It is for this reason that my joy at seeing this august assembly and being a part of it begins to be clouded by a deep sadness of doubt; because I cannot help thinking: How many of us are involved in mission in an active way?

If we appraise today the reality of Orthodox mission in the light of the Orthodox theology of mission, and the reality of our past, we must feel shame. When we are faced with the efforts and zeal of other churches in mission in Africa as against our own inactivity, knowing in most cases where these churches are leading their converts, we must shed tears. When we think, as we sometimes must do, that we have often left our brothers and sisters in the desert of mission with little or no support from us, we must regonize that repentance is called for -- a metanoia.

THE MISSION OF ORTHODOX YOUTH IN LEBANON

Ms Milia KHODR

In a region torn between third world politics and
the overwhelming modernism of the first world,
in a part of the world where, for more than a
decade, a bloody war has been raging,
in a land being drained of its youth on account of
the economic crises,
from this region which broadcast the word of the
gospel,
from this country where the religions have been
transformed into ultra-conservatism, fundamentalism
and confessionalism,
is it not necessary to re-situate and reaffirm the true
mission of Orthodoxy in the church of Antioch?

What is the mission of youngsters in the Orthodox Church of Antioch?

The church is God's privileged witness, and we are its body. Our mission is a testimony in a multi-confessional society where rapid and important permutations are taking place.

Our mission is lived in inter-personal relations, from which the Holy Spirit causes faith to be born. It is in sharing life experiences, identifying oneself with others, that the gospel can make itself understood and be communicated. Our Christ is not proclaimed on the roof-tops; he is confessed in silence.

Since the beginning of the war, we have tried in the Orthodox Youth Movement of the various church communities to react to the multiple situations in the country not as a religion, but as a church.

The mission of youth is to impel the church to remain an "ecclesia," a dual movement: from God to creation, and from the creation to God. The various religious denominations in Lebanon (and they are many: thirteen recognized by the state) have, in one way or another, manoeuvred themselves into a socio-political role.

Fortunately, Orthodoxy has stayed out of it all.

On the other hand, Orthodoxy has tried to protect its members in all parts of the country, and has hardly been interested in chalking up political gains. For this reason the Orthodox are recognized in Lebanon as being open to all. The true mission of the young people is this: to see Christ in the other person, even if he/she has another faith and other beliefs.

Faced with Islamic ultra-conservatism and fanaticism, certain churches have met them with socio-political rigidity, while claiming to speak in the name of all the Christians of Lebanon. I would like to point out that, while there is much talk in the world of Moslem fanaticism and the doings of the Islamic *Jihad*, little is heard of the similar -- and even worse -- reactions of Christians not only in Lebanon but throughout the Middle East. Before these waves of denominationalism, the Orthodox have remained disciples of the word, entering into dialogue with all parties, refraining from violence for political ends. The church is like salt, dissolved in society. True witness to Christ recognizes the uniqueness and freedom of others. As youngsters we have to continue to struggle to unify the whole of the country, and to obtain equality and justice. That is the Christian witness, a witness to a holy life.

We are struggling to preserve the church as a whole, its mission forever being "the image of his glory," seeing that there is currently a great risk of institutionalizing it.

It is splendid to live among Orthodox foundations. Our schools, social centres, universities, etc. are multiplying. But ought we to speak or dream of an Orthodox republic, as people spoke in olden times of Plato's Republic? Is it our mission to shut ourselves up in ghettos?

Orthodoxy implies an opening up nation-wide to all others. This is evident in the centres of medico-social service belonging to the Orthodox Youth Movement and the various dioceses. There, the service offered is a witness to the living God; love and service are offered in order that all may be one in Christ.

As young people, we are called upon to act for the renewal of the church. Our mission is to remain in our country despite all the difficulties, to struggle for the return of the emigrants and refugees: the Lebanese in their villages, the Palestinians in the occupied territories. We must incite the churches to unity and to a missionary vocation.

Finally, what I have presented to you is a witness to the reality both of history and of the present, narrated and handed down.

But that which I have not spoken about, and about which there is no talk, is the daily struggle of each one to stay put, the blood of thousands of martyrs in the villages, just because they had believed in the unity of the country and the brotherhood of their compatriots.

This way of living is not the object of conferences -- this silent struggle, this unwritten history through which the divine light filters, this faithfulness to the task assumed, this "*martyria*" is our mission in Lebanon:

To proclaim Christ resurrected from among the dead. "Through the resurrection, God justifies Jesus and ushers in a new era of missionary obedience until his return" (cf. Acts 1:11).

Christ is risen!

THE WITNESS OF YOUTH IN THE PARISH

Mr Constantinos PAPADAKIS

"Bless the Lord, o my soul,...
who satisfies you with good as long as you live,
so that your youth is renewed like the eagle's"(Psalm 102/3:1,5).

These lines by the king-prophet and psalm writer David are appropriate to introduce some reflections on the witness of the Orthodox youth in the life of our parish.

What follows are facts, facts from the life of a parish that for years has been struggling silently to give Christ's light through our humble powers to the souls that cry "help us" (Acts 16:9). Of course, everything was not accomplished overnight. In the youth sector, the systematic endeavour began eighteen years ago, and throughout these years the work has progressed, despite the obstacles, with God's help. The greatest proof of this progress is the continual offering of service by the youth for God and for their brothers and sisters, unhindered by time-consuming procedures and bureaucracy. Our young people's ideas are not merely respected. Our parish asks for them and gets them fulfilled. The contribution of the whole parish to the young is harmoniously combined with the active participation of the young themselves in the life of the parish.

Spiritual growth

(a) "*Parish Friendly Companies:*" These are regular weekly meetings held on weekends aiming to bind youth to the Triune God within the church. Since the parish is the cell of the church, we stress the word "parish" in the name of these companies. The young people attending our companies number more than one thousand.

To many, of course, this number may seem satisfactory, but to us it is not. And here lies a great problem: the relations between the parish and the educational staff of the district schools. There are indeed blessed teachers who come to assist the efforts of the parish and consolidate Christ in the souls of their students. Unfortunately, these cases are too rare. Then there are those teachers who do not just stay indifferent but quite openly launch atheistic and anti-ecclesiastical propaganda. This anti-church spirit, generally present in our education in recent years, affects us as well. Everything -- the presence of the priest, the Christian posters, the religious press -- is banished by the high schools, either directly or indirectly.

The devout young themseves have opened ways for solutions to this problem. They, cautiously at first and more determined later, started to turn the desk into a pulpit for Christian witness in the classroom. Outside the schoolyard (since it is forbidden inside) they regularly invite their classmates to Christian youth events. The Christian youth take an active part in the common life of their schools and, amid the political partiality of the students' communities, they present a clear, honest and peaceful Christian witness. Thus we see that many times they are respected (maybe due to fear) by teachers and classmates of opposing belief.

(b) "*Parish University:*" There is a special provision for those who finish high school, the students and post-graduate youth. For ten years we have been inviting distinguished lecturers to the "Catacomb" (bishops, Athos monks, university professors, etc.) to speak to the young on current issues.

Our parish university aims to avoid yet another problem: that of losing from our community the young finishing high school. So, besides receiving spiritual food of a deeper content, our young are given the chance to participate in the whole work of the parish. By means of new posts for responsible staff they serve in their turn within the parish.

(c) "*Parish Camps:*" Spiritual growth does not stop for the summer. Our parish offers summer camps to 120 boys and 120 girls (in two periods). Each day's program is scheduled to cover the interests and needs of the current day. It is worth noting that in the last four years we have established a "Camp Congress" especially for the high school pupils. Only the listing of the main topics shows their importance: "Economic Relations," "The Creation of the World and Creation of Humankind," "Witnessing Christ Today -- Youth and the Modern World," "Alienation."

(d) "*Youth newspaper:*" "Catacomb" is the name of a monthly newspaper produced by the high school students that began publication last December. It is a good and serious attempt and has already offered much towards Christian witness among the youth of our district. This very newspaper is a bridge used by our youth to reach the "black sheep" of Christ's flock. Dealing with currently exciting, interesting and present youth issues (drugs, modern music trends, famine, AIDS, sports and hooligans, etc.), "Catacomb" reveals that the Christian youth lives in our world and strives to transform it in Christ.

(e) "*Parishional gatherings of parents:*" Through these gatherings, parents are informed and given answers to important educational matters by experienced instructors. The generally low cultural level in this part of Thessaloniki, however, and the absence of previous experience in this field has not led to a proper stirring up of parental interest. Thus attention is now given to the younger couples and future parents. The parishional gatherings of parents are an effort to solve the problem of unity with the new families, with the whole work of the parish, since the Christian family, wholeheartedly given to the parish, is the hope of our church.

Philanthropic activity

This sector is not confined merely to the giving of alms. Let us say that the financial power of our young does not permit such a great giving margin. Love, all the same, finds ways in which to give. Quite regularly (not just on celebration days) our "Friendly Companies" organize excursions with richly entertaining programs to our district charity houses, as well as to our borderline outposts in the country.

In the arranging of exursions we could do more. It would be possible to have a more systematic planning of visits, not only to charity houses, but also to other neglected parts of the country, even work places. It is not a lack of desire or will on the part of the young, but rather a lack of time and funds plus the difficulty of moving the persons and the materials needed (costumes, musical instruments, etc.) to put on a show. Unfortunately, the financial situation of the parish does not allow the purchase of a proper vehicle for such kind of moving. For the time being, it remains a future plan to acquire a parishional vehicle and to actually render it a "vehicle of love and witness of Christ" to so many people around.

The young also play a part in our *parish blood bank*, having donated a good many of the 450 bottles collected so far.

Not least of these activities are the *free tutorial classes* that have been offered daily for ten years now by teachers and undergraduate members of this parish to the academically weak students in our schools.

Entertainment

There is no entertainment missing from the "Catacomb" that today's young people want: it is a hive of activity daily with table games such as ping-pong, etc. Quite regularly we hold video, film or slide shows.

A whole range of departments positively absorb the children's interests. There are sport clubs for the athletically-minded. For the music and song fans there are groups to teach musical instruments, an orchestra (which is continually enlarged by the addition of new instruments) and the 100-member parish youth choir. Those who wish can apprentice in one of the groups of aquarelle, class-painting, sketching, oil drawing and byzantine iconography. Up to now, these departments have organized three exhibitions of painting-iconography, quite successfully.

Our traditional Greek folklore dances have now been revived in the "Catacomb" through the efforts of the dancing teams of our folklore department. Their appearances outside the parish as well (Peraeus, Volos, Farsala, Thessaloniki) have raised enthusiastic criticism. Theatre is also one of our youth's interests. Each year the theatrical company puts on twelve plays with great success. Most importantly, these plays are written by members of the parish. The direction, scenery and costumes all come out of the youth's inventive love.

Our "Catacomb" literature group is kept going under the care of two literature teachers who are parish staff members. Those children who are talented and inclined to poetry and prose can study the works of great Greek and foreign writers. At the same time, they work a good deal on their writing, much of which is often used to make songs. We have already published the first "Anthology of Parishional Literature," and a sequel to it is underway.

We try to keep abreast of modern technological advancement: it is the third year now that our experienced staff are teaching computers. Recently, a contribution by the young helped us to buy our own computer, which we anticipate will be used extensively.

In speaking of computers and current technological advances, we should mention plans of the parish to build a radio station to operate on a non-professional basis and within the technical capacities of parish members. The aim is to pass Christ's message through the closed doors of the houses and into the people's hearts.

Everything described above is nothing but the witness of Christ in our world through a thousand tongues and in a thousand ways.

It is a fact that even the large area of the "Catacomb" has not enough space for the activities of the young. Each of the "sections" needs its own area for its activity, to store its materials and to exhibit. The problem of inadequate space has to be studied and plans for additional buildings must be made. To go outside the core of parish life, which is the church, is out of the question.

Last autumn we held an open air youth event, "Roads of Love," which moved many people, thus bringing them closer to us. It was one more bridge for the outsiders. We did not wait for them to come near. We, the Christian youth, walked in the streets singing and confessing our faith in "Christ crucified and risen." The Orthodox youthful soul cannot stay bound in a sheild of self-sufficiency and rest while all around "the harvest is plentiful, but the labourers are few" (Matt. 9:37).

It is true that a little while ago we were afraid and hesitant to step outside the "Catacomb." Now, the picture of the good Shepherd Christ seeking the one lost sheep guides and inspires us.

Liturgical life

Orthodox liturgy is the spring that brings refreshing water to our thirsty soul through the grace that fuels everything mentioned above. Orthodox liturgical life is Christ himself transfused into our veins, because "in him we live and move and have our being" (Acts 17:28).

The altar -- on which we see the book of the gospel and the chalice of life -- together with the stole of our spiritual father, are the centres around which the young people's ways of life orbit. We know well that any social work having no spiritual life, no Orthodox liturgical life, quickly vanishes. That is why our spiritual father's care and effort for the young are quite often opportunities for common liturgical life. Divine liturgies (combined at least monthly with vigils; those unique prayers in the night when everything is calm and our soul rests quietly in the touching atmosphere of the darkness), regular confession, common evening prayers and a systematic study of the Holy Fathers, make up a part of our liturgical life. Even our entertainment trips are to Orthodox monasteries and shrines in order to reinforce and consolidate the faith. Outside Greece our "pilgrimage excursions" have taken us to Constantinople, Jerusalem and Sinai, Rome, the Orthodox Centre in Geneva, Bulgaria, Romania, Yugoslavia and to the Holy Mountain of Athos.

Perhaps you wonder: why does the youth of the twentieth century, the young of the electronic era, seek refuge in parish life? What do we find here in the parish?

The parish offers us the two most valuable things that the young soul especially longs for. First, it creates a warm, humane community of persons where everyone is embraced as a brother and a sister, helps and receives help, lights and gets light. Despite human weaknesses, nobody is expelled. All, if they wish, can offer something according to their own abilities. The diakonia of the brother and sister does not require wages or bravos, nor even offices. It is given out by love for the love; a love of Christ which "does not insist on its own way" (I Cor. 13:5). To complete the human horizontal dimension is the second aspect, the communion with God. "You created us for You, Lord, and our soul agonizes till it rests in Your embrace" (St Augustin, Confessions, Book I).

In fact, the spiritual life of the parish offers rest from anxiety, water for the thirst and bread for the hunger of each soul, especially for the young. Because it is precisely the young who seek, long for the real life, with no compromise, no limitations, no false supports. Is it not, in a wrong way, the young who are seeking in the noises of lots of decibells, in the high degrees of alcohol, in the various drugs and the generally unfettered life?

The Orthodox spiritual life, under the personal instruction of the spiritual father, becomes "the wine that the reckless drank and enjoyed a lot, the sinners and changed their way, the drunkards and became fasting men, the rich and wished for poverty, the poor and got rich through hope, the simple and became wise" (St Isaac the Syrian).

The parish, as a cell of Christ's church, moves in this double God-human dimension -- the horizontal and vertical forming "the cross-way dimension" -- fascinates the young heart when it becomes a tangible reality of life. I believe that here lies the solution to the problem of the approaching and active participation of the modern youth in the body of the church.

To conclude, I ask the young people of this parish of the Announciation in Evosmos, Thessaloniki, and the young of the whole world, to unite our voices to pray with the prayer of St Basil from the divine liturgy written by him:

"Lord, educate the youth!"

WOMEN IN THE CONTEMPORARY WORLD AND THEIR MISSION IN EDUCATION

- A Case Study from Greece -

Dr Dimitra A. KOUKOURA

It is difficult to describe the role of women in contemporary society, and even more so to evaluate it accurately, without a brief survey of the role given to them in the past.

Pre-Christian convictions confined women's mission exclusively and contemptuously[1] to the biological reproduction of chiefly male offspring, and perhaps also the scheduled running of their own households. This deeply-rooted mentality, with various modifications, deviations or similarities, survives even today in certain parts of the world.[2]

Influenced by the 2000-year-old presence of Christianity[3] and marked by the radical changes in human life brought about by the industrial revolution, contemporary societies have recognized the existence in the world of a female population, capable of taking on many important roles. As a result, public life, intensely male-dominated for centuries, has been strengthened, enriched and above all completed[4] by the invaluable contribution of women.

In the Old Testament, woman is defined in terms of how useful she is to her husband; in the gospels she is a human being[5] whose value -- or lack of it -- depends on her relationship to God and to fellow human beings.[6] However, this revolutionary truth (seen against the anti-feministic attitude of the ancient world), as well as the emphatic insistence of the fathers of our church on the value of every human being,[7] have been accepted only with difficulty throughout the centuries. Social circumstances, encrusted with centuries of custom, need to be shaken by drastic and compelling external factors before they can gradually be eradicated.

Nevertheless, whatever the social circumstances -- whether the indisputable value of women is undervalued or recognized -- the calling of salvation is addressed equally to the two sexes. The whole human race, irrespective of sex, geographical origin, social position or cultural level, is called to respond positively to the divine economy. The well-known saying of the apostle Paul (Gal. 3:28) is quite clear. Male and female without distinction, when they are baptized, put on the Lord and accept his command to become holy[8] and to "go forth and make disciples of all the nations".[9]

Looking to the contemporary Greek society

In our country the local church has the particular honour of being able to date its foundation to the time of the apostles, and of including within its embrace almost the entire population.[10] Modern Greeks, therefore, are baptized in the name of the Triune God, just as their parents and all their ancestors have been with unbroken continuity for two thousand years. Nobody would dispute the truth that as many as are baptized in the name of the Holy Trinity die and are raised again together with Christ;[11] however, the sanctifying grace of God is operative only when it finds fertile soil, that is to say free human assent and responsible "synergy."[12]

In our individualistic society, it is difficult to bring people into the church, the eucharistic assembly, and only after painful suffering are they willing to learn where to find the answer to the existential agony that torments them. We still have "nations," even in a country where everything around us bears witness to the faith of centuries and to true piety. One well-known verse of our Nobel prize-winning poet speaks of the weight of our pagan heritage and the perplexity of those who have inherited it.[13] Perhaps it would be no exaggeration to extend this insight to our Orthodox tradition that surrounds us.

The architectural monuments and works of art in our museums, our popular culture and customs, and our social life, even despite the indiscriminate levelling of the industrial age, still bear witness to the unbroken identical march of the Greek people with Christianity. The more we are encircled by our Orthodox past, however, the more we are entrusted with the sacred duty of bringing it to life as a dynamic reality using contemporary forms. Otherwise, there is a great danger of lapsing into formalism, pietism, fanaticism, or even just the cultural appreciation of a distinguished past, which, however, is difficult to relate to the present.

Western civilization, to which for all our particularities we belong, can indeed boast wonderful scientific and technological achievements, but it also has patterns of life that are delusive and self-destructive. The reason has been over-emphasized as autonomous in relation to the other psychosomatic faculties, and the human being has been distorted into an individual, who, alienated in the midst of a surfeit of material goods, seeks diversion from his/her boredom and affliction. It is precisely this spirit that is penetrating our society; whereas the mission of our church is essentially not only to take under its wing those who are traditionally its children, but the whole world, and to confirm it again in the faith of the apostles, the faith of the fathers, the faith of the Orthodox.

The times, therefore, demand a general mobilization of all our resources for the pastoral work of the church, and in response to this summons it is imperative that women should meet with more appreciation of their value.

Women in the parish

In contemporary parish centres, where they operate in an organized and exemplary way, the presence of women in many fields of activity is particularly important. This in itself, however, occurs only sporadically and then is directly linked to the enlightened direction of some hierarch, who, with some of his parish clergy, has revived the institution of the parish. In our time society itself has revised the harsh attitude towards women that it held for centuries. Our church has a duty to shake off the fetters of its old social prejudices, not only to bring women into more prominence but also to underline their true meaning. The feministic west has been led either through ignorance or frustration into contradictions, disillusionment and deviations;[14] meanwhile the Orthodox east, which preserves the truth, does not have time to be absorbed in sterile contemplation of the past while ignoring the present.

Women now have many opportunities to reveal their charismatic status,[15] flowing from the church. Motherhood, the principal characteristic of their nature, in conjunction with sacramental life, is charged spiritually and can be offered eagerly to the wider pastoral work of the church. In this way, any place of work where there is a presence of women believers becomes fragrant, not only with professional conscientiousness, with punctuality in production and consequently in execution of duty, but also with understanding, discernment and consolation in interpersonal relations.

Women in education

Particularly noticeable is the female presence in all levels of education. In institutions of higher education the teaching personnel increasingly includes women in its number -- with the exception of the two faculties of theology in our country, where, according to the latest poll, only five women theologians, approximately eight percent, serve.[16] In primary and secondary education, however, women outnumber men. This is perhaps the most fertile place for passing on the message of the gospel, not only in religious education lessons but through any teaching subject.

In this circuit of communication an important role is played by the personality of the transmitter -- the teacher -- as does the way in which she communicates her knowledge and spiritual experience, and above all, the degree to which she bears in mind the contemporary context within which today's impressionable, able and also intelligent receivers -- the students -- move. More pessimistic contemporaries might say, though with some degree of superficiality, that the hope of every human society -- the youth, the best receivers of the truth -- have today been corrupted by the spirit of the age and frequently react against all that is right. The truth, perhaps, is that if there is a certain hedonistic paralysis among the youth it is due rather to the example of their elders. It would nonetheless be completely erroneous to believe that today's students lack discernment of authenticity and sensitivity to truth.

A woman teacher, and especially one in higher education who has responsibility for the adolescent age group, restless and full of readiness to criticize, is quickly rejected if she displays a lack of knowledge of her subject, or an inferiority complex, or is arrogant, presumptuous, autocratic or over-protective in her behaviour, has a sarcastic manner or is confused spiritually.

On the other hand, young people can be inspired by a woman teacher who knows her subject well and communicates with them in their own idiom and through their own preoccupations. Sincerity and reasonableness, breadth, understanding and above all love, which is a reflection of her own spiritual life, cannot fail to make an impression on the students, however much in today's classrooms, especially in the cities, they may seem indifferent and frequently disturbed.

An enlightened woman educator can gain the trust of the young people, understand their worries, advise them in their activities and perhaps even, by presenting a stable and blameless witness -- if other supporting factors also make their contribution, -- lead them into the sacramental eucharistic communion.

NOTES

1. Savvas Agourides, Ho Iesous kai hai gynaikes, in *Deltion Biblikôn Meletôn* 2(1981), p. 64 (including rich bibliography).

2. In our case, characteristic examples of this mentality are the classic essays of contemporary Greek literature by Alexandros Papadiamandes ("*He phonissa,*" The Murderess) and by Andreas Karkavitsas ("*Ho zetianos,*" The Begger). Another source of rich information on the subject is the doctoral dissertation of Anthoula Sepheriadou, *Hoi gynaikeies morphes eis to ergo tou K. Chatzopoulou*, Ioannena 1982.

3. Cf. Rosa Imbriotis, *He gynaika eis to Byzantio*, Athenai.

4. Cf. Paul Evdokimov, *La femme et le salut du monde*, Paris, Casterman, 1958, pp. 245-6: "Le masculin et le féminin sont antinomiques. Cela veut dire que dans l'ordre naturel ils sont incompatibles. Ils ne se révèlent complémentaires que dans l'ordre de la grâce, en Christ."

5. Savvas Agourides, op. cit., p. 65. For Jesus the woman has a value in herself. The particular interest Jesus showed for women was not a condescendence: for him men and women are perfectly equal.

6. Matthew 25:4.

7. Gregory Nazianzus, *Sermo 37,6*, in MPG 36,298B: "Laws are against women, for those who prepared them were man."

8. I Peter 1:15.

9. Matthew 28:19.

10. That means ninety-seven percent of the population; the other three percent represents Greek citizens having a different origin (Muslims, Jews, etc.).

11. II Timothy 2:11.

12. Gregory Palamas, *Sermo 16*, in MPG 151:200D-201A.

13. Cf. G. Sepheris, *Mythistorema II*, Athenai 1964, p. 151.

14. Cf. Paul Evdokimov, op. cit., pp. 263-4: "La virilisation de la femme vise à modifier son type anthropologique, à la rendre intérieurement, dans sa psyché, identique par nature à l'homme. Ce projet de nivellement décèle

la lutte la plus virulente contre la loi de Dieu car c'est l'anéantissement de l'état charismatique féminin."

15. Cf. Paul Evdokimov, op. cit., p. 221: "A l'opposé de tout égalitarisme et révendication, c'est le rayonnement le plus naturel de son état charismatique. C'est le ministère du Paraclet, la grâce de consolation et de joie, et qui postule l'être féminin en tant que mère pour qui tout être est son enfant."

16. Cf. Eftihias Youltsi, *Expériences et vues d'une théologienne orthodoxe concernant au choix d'études théologiques et sa relation avec la théologie et l'Eglise de Grèce*, p. 3; 30 Colloquio "Teologi Laici nelle Chiese Cristiane," 24-26 Avrile 1987, Facoltá di Teologia di Sicilia, Palermo.

WOMEN IN MISSION

- An Experience from Egypt -

Sister Agapie ASAAD

Organized groups, individuals, monks, clergymen, merchants, soldiers and devout women from Egypt went out to almost all parts of the world and spread the gospel. Early missionary activities were not only evangelistic but were also social developments and charitable deeds.

The first story to be shared here is that of the men of the Theban Legion, and a nurse whose name was Verena. As Egypt was ruled by the Romans, the latter mobilized Egyptian youth to serve in their army. One of the Egyptian legions was known as the Theban Legion (6600 Egyptian soldiers) because its members were natives of Thebes, capital of Pharaonic Egypt (present day Luxor).

In Europe (Switzerland), the Theban Legion[1], led by Maurice, watered the land with their blood of martyrdom when they refused to sacrifice to the gods. Hence, the place was called St Moritz. Verena, the lady nurse, was not killed. She spent the rest of her life in present day Switzerland, educating the people to become Christians and at the same time, teaching them the principles of hygiene. To this day, her icon depicts her holding a water jug in one hand and a comb in the other. There is a statue of her erected in the garden of the Swiss Consulate in Cairo.

A contemporary Swiss journalist, writing about her not so long ago, related her amazing story and said that through her consecration and devoted Christian service, Verena, native of Garagonz in Upper Egypt and one-time nurse, became the matron saint of housewives and the healer of lepers in Switzerland[2].

Felix, his sister Regula and Exuperantius their friend, spread the gospel to Zurich; and the official seal of the country of Zurich still carries the picture of the three Coptic evangelists.

Christianity was first introduced into Axum (Ethiopia) from Egypt by merchants through their commercial and maritime relations. St Athanasius, the XXth Pope of Alexandria, ordained Frumentius Bishop of Ethiopia in 330. For sixteen centuries Egypt, the See of St Mark the evangelist, continued to send bishops to Ethiopia.

Two observations are worth mentioning here:

1) *Kerygma, leitourgia, martyria, koinonia, diakonia* are some of the aspects of the Coptic Orthodox churches' faith and tradition. They belong together and form the heart of Orthodox witness. They are expressions of the life of the church witness to the gospel events. Basically, church education is to care for all human beings and for every aspect of the human being; education, economics, housing, etc., in the urban and rural areas among educated and non- educated. Christian education in the home is becoming indispensible.

2) Women are not less involved in mission at home and abroad. They are trained to face the various needs of the people. Today there are twenty deaconesses houses in fifteen dioceses in Egypt. They offer educational, medical and social services. Some of them were sent by their churches to do mission abroad, mainly in Ethiopia, Kenya and the USA.

I would like to speak about a particular experience of being a partner in mission to Ethiopia. In 1972, an invitation from the Ethiopian Orthodox Church came to a Coptic Orthodox community, "The Daughters of St Mary Convent" in Beni

Souef, with the wish to work together. One of the sisters lived six years under the past and present regime at a convent of sisters near Addis Ababa.

Having received the blessings of His Holiness, Pope Shenouda III, and Metropolitan Athanasios of Beni Souef, the sister left her country. She was warmly received and welcomed by His Grace Habte Marian, the Dean of the Holy Trinity Cathedral and spiritual father of a convent of active sisters.

Her assignments were:

> (a) to teach English literature and Christian education to a convent school for Christian and non-Christian students; (b) to offer first aid treatment to students and labourers at the convent farm; (c) to prepare Christian literature in English for twelve grades (the programs were put together by Oriental Orthodox churches); (d) to do secretarial work for two homes of children and adults who came from drought districts and provinces, many of whom were non-Christians; (e) to share liturgical and communal life with the sisters and students; (f) to conduct Sunday School classes for Egyptian expatriates in Addis Ababa.

The sister adjusted quickly to the different culture and tradition, food and climate through the love and care of the Ethiopian friends. She was always conscious of her role as a partner in mission. The mission in Jesus and we are working together. Both of us are receiving and giving. After a few months she joined a language institute to study the national language and after one year she was able to speak like a native. She shared their pain and sufferings in many small ways. She also rejoiced with the fruits of the work, which is being blessed by God. In 1970 the number of sisters was thirteen; it has now grown to thirty sisters and twenty novices.

- The number of children helped from drought provinces is 203, it was seventy-five in 1929.

- The convent school results have been and are still the top ones in the town.

- A bakery and fruit shop are run by the sister for the town since bread is scarce.

- Several sisters received further education in Europe (England, Germany and Italy).

- A vocational training centre for graduate students coming from ordinary schools was created.

- Fourteen men labourers left the work on the farm and the sister/convent girls took over. Productivity is increasing far more than before.

The Coptic Orthodox Church in Egypt and the Ethiopian Orthodox Church have long histories of friendship and partnership in mission. We in Egypt are making preparations to receive Ethiopian sisters.

NOTES

1. City of Zurich Archives.

2. *Journal Suisse d'Egypte et du Proche Orient* No 37 of the 23rd year in Alexandria on September 14, 1949; also *Lexique historique de la Suisse*, under the names Soleure & Zuzach.

THE ORTHODOX MISSION IN THE FAR EAST

Fr. Sotirios TRAMBAS

I. Present situation

Today, under the *aegis* of the Ecumenical Patriarchate, in the province of the Metropolis of New Zealand, a missionary effort is being undertaken by the "Eastern Orthodox Mission." This organ, established by the Ecumenical Patriarchate, has its centre in Seoul (Korea), and is recognized by the Korean authorities.

Korea

Privately-owned Orthodox churches are serving in Seoul, Pusan and Inchon. In the town of Chonsu, a chapel functions in a hired hall. There are active groups of Orthodox believers in the village of Palangni and in the town of Taegou, where land has been bought and the construction of churches is awaited.

In the above-mentioned churches there are four priests holding services; two of them are Greeks and the other two are Koreans. Periodically, voluntary priests come from Greece for a period of several months.

Each church has its own schools of catechism (at all levels, from kindergarten age up to secondary school age), its youth clubs and charitable societies. During the winter and summer holidays, there are special catechetical programmes for Orthodox students and young people, as well as those designed to attract non-Christians to the Orthodox faith. Also in Seoul, Pusan and Inchon are seminaries for the training of catechists and missionary collaborators. Since 1982 a theological seminary, running two-year courses for catechists, and four-year courses for preachers and clergymen, has been operative.

A continuous effort is being made to translate and set to music the various worship services, to publish handbooks for catechism (catechetical materials), and materials on Orthodox spirituality, patristic texts, lessons for the theological seminary, newsletters on Orthodoxy, etc.

Those who wish to be baptized follow a special course of lessons lasting several months, or years, according to circumstances. Catechumens also have to study the book of Orthodox catechism edited especially for them.

Recently a monastery was erected, some sixty kms from Seoul, which will serve as a convent for nuns. It is expected that the first three Orthodox nuns will move in there very soon after travelling from Greece.

India

An Orthodox mission was started some eight years ago by Archimandrite Athanasios Anthidis in West Bengal. The missionary centre is in the town of Arambach, 104 kms from Calcutta. There is a church, a rectory, a hostel and a printing shop. The Indian priest, who holds a degree in English literature, has -- with the help of his assistants -- translated into Bengali the Great Euchologion, the main worship services, the Orthodox catechism, a history of the Orthodox church and other essential Orthodox works.

Under the guidance of the Greek priest responsible for the mission, a seminary for catechists and priests is functioning. The Orthodox community has been recognized by the state. A second Orthodox church -- at present just a straw hut -- has been opened in a village twenty-five kms from Arambach, and is served by the second Indian priest.

There are active groups of Orthodox in two other villages; the two chaplains take turns in visiting them to hold services.

Preparation of catechumens for baptism is undertaken not only by the two priests, but also by the specially trained catechists.

Hong Kong

A mission was started recently in Hong Kong, with a dual purpose: (1) to meet the religious needs of the Orthodox residents; (2) to attract the local people to Orthodoxy. An Orthodox chapel has been temporarily created in the home of the first Orthodox Chinese. It is served by priests travelling there periodically from Seoul and Greece.

The Orthodox community has been recognized by the local authorities, and experienced women catechists, who have taught Orthodox religious classes in the USA, give lessons to the children.

A few active Orthodox groups exist, as follows: (a) in Manila, where a small Orthodox church has been built; (b) in Singapore, where the Armenian church is used for worship; (c) in Jakarta, where services are held by visiting Greek priests.

In addition to the priests, all the above Orthodox communities are periodically visited by His Eminence the Metropolitan of New Zealand, acting as Exarch of the Ecumenical Patriarchate.

II. Plans for the future

Korea

- Ordination of native priests to serve the churches in Korea and other regions of Asia.
- Strengthening the mission by sending priests from Greece.
- Staffing the convent and developing Orthodox monasticism in the region.
- Building of churches in Chonju, Taegu and Palangni, as well as in other towns.
- Editing patristic texts.

- Use of mass media to spread Orthodoxy.
- Holding open air missionary meetings.
- Adapting hymns, church architecture and painting in accordance with local cultural traditions.
- Working towards the recognition of the Theological Seminary by an Orthodox theological faculty.
- Staff training.

Hong Kong

- Acquiring a privately-owned Orthodox church.
- Installing a permanent priest.
- Running a systematic mission.
- Translating the main worship services into Cantonese.

India

- The establishment of a Greek Orthodox church in Calcutta and the establishment of a mission.
- The investment of the church's income in various projects, both catechetical and philanthropic (an orphanage, an old people's home).
- Erecting churches in regions where there are active Orthodox native groups.
- Ordination of Indian priests, and reinforcement of the mission by priests from other Orthodox countries.
- Translation of Orthodox books.

Indonesia

An Indonesian priest-cum-theologian is ready to undertake missionary work in Java as from June 1988. He has already translated the divine liturgy, vespers and matins. In the meantime, three other Indonesians are studying at the Theological School in Boston, Massachusetts.

A church and missionary centre are needed to develop the mission.

III. The Patriarchal Foundation for the Far East Orthodox Mission

The Patriarchal Foundation for the Far East Orthodox Mission, created by the Ecumenical Patriarchate, has its offices in Athens and is expected to be recognized soon by the Greek Government. In collaboration with other missionary bodies, its aim is to systematize aid and assistance to the missionary effort being made in the Far East. It also plans to inform Orthodox churches throughout the world about the Orthodox communities existing in the Far East, so that Orthodox travelling in Far Eastern countries may know where they can attend services and keep in touch with the Orthodox church, and also encourage their acquaintances from the region to come into contact with the Orthodox Church. (It is a known fact that merchants from the Far East brought the gospel to Rome.)

The Patriarchal Foundation will mobilize clergy to offer their services either on a permanent basis or periodically to Orthodox communities not yet having native priests. It will also prepare sung hymns, handbooks for catechism, Orthodox texts to broaden the spiritual awareness of the faithful, with the aim of facilitating their translation into the local languages by on-the-spot collaborators of the mission.

The Foundation will serve to encourage distinguished volunteer theologians to travel to the sessions for conferences, organize seminars to fortify the collaborators and the faithful in general, publicize the Orthodox presence in these countries (press, radio and television interviews), to train native theologians to teach in the theological seminary.

ORTHODOXY IN MISSION

- Reflections and Perspectives from an African Experience -

Bishop Antonios MARCOS

Pastoral work and mission

In one of his epistles, St John Chrysostom said that there are two kinds of bishops: the one, who is a pastoral bishop and cares for his parish, would say: "My parish is my universe"; the other, who is a missionary bishop, would rather affirm: "The universe is my parish." It seems that St John Chrysostom was very much oriented toward the latter. On another occasion he said, "We have to preach because we have a full vineyard to carry and a full world to evangelize."

So when we look at external mission, we should understand that even those who are in their parishes, be they bishops or priests, have a mission; they have to be mission-oriented, always keeping in mind their responsibility to evangelize others out of the circle of their own parish.

Cross-cultural mission

Let us recall what the Book of Revelation says: "I looked, and behold, a great multitude which no man could number, from every nation, from all tribes and peoples, and tongues, standing before the throne and before the Lamb, clothed in white robes with palm branches in their hands" (7:9).

What does this mean in terms of mission? Our churches -- in Thessaloniki, in Athens, or anywhere -- appear the same: identical icons and architecture, similar songs and language. Thus, we could say that, through time and space, the life of our churches is based on the same model. However, when this similarity is generalized to the extent that we still use the same model today in the USA or in Kenya or in Australia, we risk the danger of "modality." By modality I mean in this context sterile repetition, the lack of any spiritual revival.

Younger and older faithful, as well as people from the periphery of the church (and, I am tempted to add, even people from the periphery of the periphery), express today in various ways and on several occasions their love for Christ, their willingness to carry the church, their readiness to abandon their culture and language, their neighbours and parents, their tribes and nations. They want to sacrifice their peaceful existence and be as soldiers. They are ready to go beyond any barrier and become involved in a "cross-cultural mission." A serious question comes to mind: What are the real possibilities offered today to these people by our churches?

I had the privilege of being asked to serve my small village, where Christian and non-Christian communities are living together. Even the more practical aspect of my work, i.e., sitting on the floor to discuss with people, was enough to think about the cross-cultural nature of my work. Inspite of all kinds of inconveniences, I loved this service because I had the opportunity to be with people who were forgotten and nobody was asking about them. A little later I had another cross-cultural experience when I went to Ethiopia and met people of different cultures and language, although we belong to the same church tradition. What can I say about the difficulties? One has to live them. But in spite of all, I found myself ready to do mission work in this spirit.

Preaching the gospel today

We become more aware of the necessity of such work when we realize that two-thirds of our world have never heard about our Lord Jesus Christ. The real problem for us is not if these brothers and sisters are ready to accept the Bible but rather how to go and meet them where they are and how to involve ourselves in what can be called a cross-cultural mission, a mission in Christ's way.

In his epistle to the Romans, St Paul says that "every one who calls upon the name of the Lord will be saved" (10:13). How can they call on a name they have never had the opportunity to know? How can they hear without anyone speaking to them? And those who would be ready to preach, could they do so unless they are sent and able to say how beautiful are the deeds of those who believe in Jesus?

The Lord reminded his apostles that he was the harvest and they were the labourers (cf. Matt 9:37 and Luke 10:2). These verses have been discussed in the mission work of all our churches and have created productive ideas for evangelism. They are, I believe, the verses that prompt us to emphasize in this gathering the importance of external mission.

Mission and revival

Undoubtedly, sending people to external mission is a sign of revival of the whole church. Recently I had a discussion with an Orthodox brother from the USA who told me that his church sends young people to Kenya to participate in mission and development work. "There must have been a revival in your church," I said to him. "Very true," he replied. "Because when our young people come back they contribute much to the life, the growth and the spirituality of the church."

In fact, when we are limited -- I would even say imprisoned -- in our respective communities, parishes or churches, all our energy goes to fight each other and to struggle with each other on the local level. Our faith and our spirituality, however, demand continuous movement: gathering into one body, going outside to serve God's creatures and coming back again.

Our outgoing movement has to be seen not only in relation to those who have not yet been evangelized but also to the Christian brothers and sisters from our communities and churches. We are not allowed to jealously keep our apostolic roots for ourselves. We must share the riches of our apostolicity with our brothers and sisters throughout the world. We have also to challenge our apostolicity with today's reality, which is the authenticity and originality of many Christian communities and churches.

A new experience

Our church, the Coptic Orthodox Church, received in 1932 an appeal from the African Independent Churches, which knew vaguely that there was an apostolic Christianity in the north of the continent. These churches were indigenous churches separated from "the church of the white man." They were looking for an ancient and original African theology. They knew the existence of the Coptic Orthodox Church, they even knew the word "coptic" but without being able to give real content to it.

Unfortunately at that time our church was not ready to answer this request, for various reasons. The African Independent Churches, however, did not lose their hope and came back again reminding us of the need for contacts, exchange in love and mutual understanding.

A new mission situation, therefore, is before us. This is a form of external mission for which we all are responsible. The facts are there. It is up to us to collect more information, proceed to a careful analysis of the whole situation and humbly offer our assistance.

To give you an example, in order to better understand these brothers and sisters from the African Independent Churches, I stayed alongside them for thirteen hours while they celebrated and danced. I had a Bible and a prayerbook in my pocket; I wanted to share church history and theology with them, but I soon realized that what I had to do first was to hear them, to know them, to understand them, to discover that their faith and their worship -- so different from our worship -- come from their hearts and their minds, their souls and their spirits.

Some practical recommendations

I have attempted here to touch on some points of our work that seem significant to me and that could be used to help us formulate some practical recommendations.

What is needed above all is focus to share our mission experiences, to learn from each other, to walk together towards the same goal. We could form a team that would be responsible for giving and receiving news from missions and analyzing from various perspectives some facts and realities related to our mission efforts. This would be particularly constructive for our mission work and, at the same time, would bring us closer to each other.

We have a good number of qualified Orthodox missionaries whose experience should be used by our churches. Our theological schools and other educational institutes should emphasize missiological studies and invite missionaries to teach. The incorporation of missiology to programs of theological education would help to develop the skills needed for mission work and to prepare candidates for it.

It is not enough, however, to think only about theological education. Programs for mission awareness should also be organized for parishes, Bible study circles and Sunday schools, so that the missionary vocation becomes a main concern in the life of our churches. The minimum our faithful can do is to be aware of our efforts and to pray for us.

Priests, bishops, archbishops, metropolitans, patriarchs and holy synods have also to be informed about our work and sensitized to the imperative of mission today. Monks and nuns could also be of great help in our task for many of them are very willing to be involved in external mission, and monastic witness is of prime importance to any mission work.

Finally, why should we not establish an institute, an Institute for Missiology? It could bring people together and give them the necessary education for mission work. It is not enough to spell out the importance of mission for our churches; we must also prepare ourselves by creating the appropriate structures and institutions in order to prepare ourselves for concrete needs and situations.

These are some dreams that I wanted to share with you, hoping that our consultation, after thorough discussion and deep reflection, would strongly recommend the fulfilling of them to our respective churches for the sake of our witness within the contemporary world.

(Resumé from a taped recording.)

ORTHODOXY IN MISSION

- The Alaskan Experience -

Fr Michael OLEKSA

In the process of evangelization, both those who evangelize and those who receive the gospel are enriched, transformed and renewed. The process of achieving the twin goals of all authentic Orthodox mission is:

1) making the fullness of the Orthodox tradition "incarnate" in a new culture by adapting its language, culture, and, insofar as possible, its traditions and customs, "baptizing" them into the church;

2) establishing eventually a self-governing church with its own indigenous clergy, spirituality and mission, which has positive effects on the entire church.

I present here a few missiological principles derived from the historical experiences of the Orthodox Church in Alaska.

Following the European discovery of Alaska in 1741, Siberian frontiersmen ventured regularly into the Aleutian Islands, many remaining permanently and settling down with Alaskan wives, raising Alaskan children and thus serving as the first evangelists as they baptized their families. When the first missionaries arrived from Valamo, Finland, in September 1794, they discovered that most of the Aleutian Island people were already "Christian," but in need of a more sophisticated religious education. Father Herman, a lay monk, remained at his hermitage on Spruce Island near Kodiak and served by showing through the example of his holy life what a Christian can and should be. Although he operated a school, and later an orphanage, his mission was essentially one of personal holiness. In 1824, Father John (later Metropolitan Innocent) developed a writing system and began translation into Aleut languages, founded several schools, built two churches, and evangelized indigenous tribes on both sides of the Bering Sea. From this foundation of Christian holiness and education sprang two generations of native Alaskan lay missionaries who were responsible not only for the survival but also the growth of the Orthodox Church in Alaska, especially after the colony was sold to the United States in 1867, and almost all Siberian clergy had returned to Russia. The diocesan centre was eventually transferred to San Francisco as immigrants from Europe and later the Middle East began to arrive in the United States. In this way Alaska became the "mother diocese" of the Orthodox Church in America.

In Alaska, Aleut clergy, and especially laity, were actively engaged in strengthening and extending the mission, particularly in continuing the translation of biblical and liturgical texts, some of which, like the gospels of Mark, Luke and John and the Acts of the Holy Apostles, were published by the mission with funds contributed by the Aleut faithful themselves. Others, which had circulated orally for generations, were passed from translator to choir, from village to village, especially among the Eskimos. Entire congregations sang the services by heart, and continued to gather for worship, ninety percent of them without clergy, for many decades.

This success derives from the application of certain fundamental principles:

1) The services must be celebrated in an intelligible language.

2) There must be continuing education and explanation of the scripture and the liturgical and sacramental rites (Eskimo services usually include two or even three sermons, preached mostly by lay readers and catechists ("chiefs").

3) Lay involvement and responsibility are basic to the success of any missionary effort. One might even say that the shepherd, the pastor, tends the flock but the growth, the multiplication of the sheep, depends essentially on the effort, the desire and energy of the flock itself, together with the grace and will of the Father who draws whom he will to Christ.

Besides these lessons in missiological approach, which the Alaskan experience offers us, there is another dimension of this church's spirituality that must be mentioned, however briefly and inadequately. Native Americans possess a deep appreciation and indeed a spiritual apprehension of the natural world, the entire created universe, its beauty and goodness. Our church affirms this liturgically in various sacramental acts, in numerous hymns and prayers, and celebrations (for example, the Great Blessing of Water of Theophany). The secular intelligentsia, especially in the west, seems drawn to various Oriental religious traditions and movements, precisely because these offer a wholistic, integrated experience and vision of reality, which has largely been lost in western Christian expressions, but, by God's grace and mercy, has been to a large extent presented within the traditions of the Christian east. This created a bridge, and later an inner bond with indigenous peoples of America, and presents the Orthodox churches with a remarkable missionary opportunity today.

THE ROLE OF THE PARISH IN MISSION

Fr Alexandros KALPAKIDIS

"Do the work of an evangelist,
fulfil your ministry" (II Tim. 4:5).

Our parish

The parish of the Announciation at Evosmos is a characteristic example of evangelistic witness in a place that, within the last fifteen years, has undergone a booming development in terms of population, economy and culture.

When I was appointed here in 1970 as the rector of the church of St Athanasios, Evosmos was a marginal suburb of the major district of Thessaloniki, populated by white and blue collar workers, farmers and minor businessmen. It looked like a small provincial town without any particular spiritual or cultural life. While in the city centre of Thessaloniki the university and various other institutions had always stirred vigorous cultural activity, here the improvement in the standard of living, the increase in income, the acquiring of newly-built houses, the education of the children were the major interests. It was a place investing all its present activities in hope of a better future.

Today, eighteen years later, we witness the realization of that dream. The area has started to flourish. Modern housing has replaced the old, the economic situation is much better, the young generation enjoys a higher level of education, with a large number of students and post-graduates of the university faculties. As a result of this there has been development of spiritual interests and cultural activities.

Naturally enough, new problems have appeared together with the spectacular uprising. The western way of life influences the population -- especially the young -- and alienates them from the values of their past, as it attracts through television and the cafeterias an infinitely affluent society, a materialistic life that aims at pleasures, including even the "mysterious" experience of drugs.

This western type of materialistic life is often accompanied by a marxist kind of materialistic attitude, and this appears not to be a revolution but a fashion that is projected and supported too by modern Greek thinkers.

Amid this quickly-growing and variable social environment, the pastoral and missionary activity at our parish started with the apostolic experience of becoming acquainted with the "person of Christ" and communicating with him in the worship, the sacraments, and especially the divine liturgy. The altar became the centre of the parish, the heart that feeds the sacred blood of life to all the believers, as holy eucharist is the ground on which the entire church stands.

According to Orthodox tradition and ecclesiology, the most primal factor for the formation of the whole structure and growth of the parish is the bishop who stands "in place and type" of Christ. So this has been and remains the plan upon which we work and act: Christ-church-bishop-parish-rector. Because, in the Orthodox tradition and teaching, "church is not called" without the bishop, according to St Ignatius (Tral. 3:7) and "wherever the bishop appears, there may the people be" (Smyrn. 8:3).

Under these circumstances and with the blessing of our own bishop, we had to turn to new methods of evangelism and mission experiences, using all the new possibilities, identifying and trying to face the new problems that became evident.

Today we can confirm that our efforts have produced some impressive fruit and that the speed of the development in church life surpassed by far the relevant speed of increase in the worldly life of this place.

Some of our efforts

In the past, the small parish church was the centre of a feeble Christian presence, limited to answering the basic religious demands of a people with no particular spiritual interest. Today, the new large church is the emblem of Evosmos, the centre of a spiritual activity that has a great influence on the social life and is the refuge shelter for each soul seeking peace.

The story of our church itself is an illustration of the continually escalating activity of the parish.

In 1970 there was just the old, small and low church of St Athanasios, by the graveyard. Situated on the margin of life, a guardian of the dead, away from the eyes of the living, it had a rare congregation of old-age pensioners waiting for their time to leave this world. No presence of the young, no liveliness. The church did not have a part in the life of the place. On the contrary, there was considerable activity on the part of the Jehovah's Witnesses.

Yet, the place lived in the present looking forward to the hope of a better future. A similar hope, based solely on faith in Christ, has led us to start working in that desperate situation. We tried, however, to never forget that "suffering produces endurance, and endurance produces character, and character produces hope, and hope does not disappoint us, because God's love has been poured into our hearts through the Holy Spirit which has been given to us" (Rom. 5:3-5).

The endeavour had two dimensions, which are the basis of Orthodoxy. One dimension refers to the past, the beauty of our Orthodoxy's treasures, anything beautiful and true given through liturgical life, byzantine arts, the lives and the writings of the saints. The second dimension refers to the future, incarnated by the youth, the strength of the youth that receive the baton ready to thrust themselves into struggles with far-reaching aims. If we keep in mind that the past starts with Christ and that the future leads to Christ, the *alpha* and *omega* (Rev. 1:8), we realize that church life has to be harmoniously combined in past and present and future, so as not to diminish Christ who is "the same yesterday and today and for ever" (Heb. 13:8).

We have tried to project the heritage of the past mainly through liturgical life. We took pains so that the divine liturgy and the sacraments would express the beauty of Orthodoxy, offer peace to the souls and talk to them. In sermons, at daily services, on Sundays and great celebrations, we explained the spirituality of Orthodoxy, always in reference to modern human beings and their problems. The word of God has become the everyday seed in the vineyard of the parish. The word, i.e., the sermon, and the liturgical life, combined with praying and intense spiritual concentration, led us towards the communion of the Holy Trinity and the true communion of the saints.

In the same spirit, we organized the catechism schools in the parish, with a teaching staff of young men and women of the parish who soon joined our efforts. We established special divine liturgies for school children. We attempted to distribute widely Christian literature and counteract the Jehovah's Witnesses' activity by organizing centres for studying the Bible. Special attention was given to confession, for the repentance of a sinful life for believers of all ages.

Within a short time, the congregation attendance increased so much that the church of St Athanasios could not suffice. Many people had to stay outside in the church-yard. The building of a new church was an inevitable demand, so we began to construct the present church, the Church of the Announciation. Not wishing to work in vain, we asked the Lord to be the "first builder," since "unless the Lord builds the house, those who build it labour in vain" (Psalm 126/7:22).

The building of the church underwent two periods, reminding us of the advance of the church in the history of the world.

We started with the underground place, which although conveniently large, is well enough under the surface of the ground. We call it the *Catacomb* to remind us of the heroic period of the ancient church which started its way scorned by the world but beloved by God. In this *Catacomb* we have known fights and efforts. We have lived joys and grievances that joined us tightly with the common aim of Christ conquering Evosmos. We have had touching cooperation and support from people who proved themselves invaluable workers and who are continuously sacrificing themselves for the true needs of the parish. For all of them, we can repeat what St Paul, the Apostle of the Nations, writes of his fellow-workers: they have been helpers of many and of myself as well, and risked their necks for my life (cf. Rom. 16:2-4). In grateful recognition of all these tireless workers, each day on the celebration of Sts Akyla and Priscilla, fellow-workers of St Paul (13 February), we have a spiritual gathering to honour in the person of the saints the valuable workers of the parish.

As the congregation increased, the catechism schools developed and the Christian youth grew numerous. The effort to build the church was hampered by lack of funds. The place was poor. We tried every means of raising money. The children of the primary schools offered their money from the carol singing at Christmas which helped to build the dome of the church. We even gathered and accumulated paper to sell for recycling. Each year the parish women prepare handicrafts, celebration cards, lotteries, and organize funeral receptions. Together, young and old, they sell rolls, flowers and hold yearly collections of contributions.

So, little by little, the Church of the Announciation rose commanding and beautiful, the best building in Evosmos and the pride of its inhabitants. This reminds us the period when the church rose from the catacombs wearing "as crimson robe the blood of the martyrs" and amazed the people with its beauty. We all felt a great spiritual uplift when we heard our bishop and spiritual father, H.E. Metropolitan Dionysios, say on the day of the opening (9 May 1982), "The Father has built this house; the Son has fixed this house; the Holy Spirit has renovated this house, enlightening and supporting and making saints of our souls."

Nowadays, we live an intense liturgical life in this church. Our people especially love the vigils, when in a mystical atmosphere we "lift up our hands to the holy place, and bless the Lord" (Psalm 133/4:2). Here we live the triumph of the church and "the image" becomes "in the likeness" of God.

As well as "the sacrament of the blood," which is the heart of our liturgy, there is "the sacrament of the word," which we also try to celebrate continuously. So, the word of God never ceases to be heard, winter and summer, during Sunday and weekday celebrations, in the church and in the "home churches," especially in the thirteen houses scattered throughout the parish where members of the parish operate as branches of the spiritual centre for the study of the Bible.

Finally, for the benefit of all those who are not active members in its life and activities, the parish produces a bi-monthly bulletin. Called *Parish Breath*, this bulletin (3,000 copies) serves to update all the faithful of Evosmos.

Looking towards the future

What are our prospects for the future? What is there in store to follow? There is a lot to be done. We know that love must always seek and find new ways. "We have got as a duty to serve diakonia" goes a song of our young, and this is our daily conscientious task.

The Lord chose the apostles "to be with him, and to be sent out to preach, and to have authority to cast out demons" (Mark 3:14-15). In this line we can clearly see the three directives of the pastoral and evangelistic work:

1. Staying with Christ: *worship and liturgy;*
2. Solidarity for the fellow human being: *diakonia;*
3. Preaching the truth: *witness.*

We have known that this diakonia of the material and the spiritual needs not only of the pain but of the joy as well, is the most important alms we can offer our brothers and sisters: "rushing to make brothers see reason, this is the first of the alms" imitating the "master of the alms" Jesus Christ himself who, according to St John Chrysostom "become what you were, so that you would become what you were not, due to mercy."

We fight to offer this diakonia to all with no discrimination, no conditions and limitations, obeying the invitation to "bear one another's burdens" (Gal. 6:2) and "welcome one another" (Rom. 15:7) putting up with "the failings of the weak" (Rom. 15:1).

We want our diakonia to enlighten the human mind and influence social life through a ray of Christian love and hope, to announce the great mercy of God in a merciless society of egotism and rivalry, of war against everything and everybody. Not, for sure, to turn the parish into a heaven on earth but to prevent it from becoming a hell.

To mention some of our specific future plans: the completing of the work on the church and the parish house for the elderly, the building of a new spiritual and cultural centre properly equipped (rooms for conferences, parish museum, etc.), the acquisition of our own property to build a camp and to able to accept many more children as well as parents and persons of the third age, the computerized recording of the entire property of the parish, and the establishment of a regular bookshop.

Through all of this, our prime target, our only target, is the offering of salvation to human souls through the giving of the "life-giving and purest sacrament" so that now the "company of those who believe is of one heart and soul" (Acts 4:32) and the whole parish may be "transplanted" in the kingdom of God.

In this diakonia, we try to experience living the invitations of St Paul: "Let love be genuine; hate what is evil, hold fast to what is good; love one another with brotherly affection; outdo one another in showing honour. Never flag in zeal, be aglow with the Spirit, serve the Lord. Rejoice in your hope, be patient in tribulation, be constant in prayer. Contribute to the needs of the saints, practise hospitality" (Rom. 12:9-13).

We ask you to pray to God for his blessing on our spiritual struggle as, "From him and through him and to him are all things. To him be glory for ever. Amen" (Rom. 11:36).

THREE

"AFTERWORDS"

The final words are from three participants, experiencing for the first time an Orthodox gathering of this nature.

The three -- a young Kenyan Orthodox priest, an Orthodox woman from Greek academic circles and a Presbyterian minister from the USA -- offer their reflections on the consultation as follows.

A learning experience

Much has been done and still more effort is being applied by the Commission on World Mission and Evangelism of the World Council of Churches to try to deepen the whole concept of "Mission in Christ's Way."

What I particularly appreciated about the Orthodox Consultation in Neapolis was the presence of young African priests and lay persons who took part and represented their Patriarchate. Not only were they given the opportunity to experience the universality of the Orthodox Church but also they were challenged then to take back the message to their brothers and sisters in Africa. May I say that this consultation was an education for us; all that we took away with us was of great importance, especially in carrying out the mission work of our young African Church.

May Almighty God enlighten all of us in our missionary efforts.

Fr Paul Njoroge Gathuru
Mathathia - Kenya

A polyphony without discord

The presence of delegates from almost all Eastern Orthodox and Oriental Orthodox churches at the consultation on Orthodox mission, held in Neapolis, brought a fresh understanding of Orthodox missionary work, allowing the participating churches to realize that methodological differences and cultural peculiarities do not affect the theological dimension of mission, and are therefore not only admissible but even sought after, as they create greater flexibility and a better use of the various local cultural elements.

The local Orthodox churches differ considerably from each other in their social and cultural backgrounds as well as in their political and economic environments, a fact that is clearly reflected in their conception of evangelistic and mission work, because mission is the field par excellence where the cultural riches of both those offering and those receiving God's message contribute to the final result. The experience and methods of each local church involved in missionary work are therefore unique despite identical aims. Doing mission is a very complicated process and it is natural that every local church tends to transmit its own social and cultural parameters. At the Neapolis Consultation all these approaches were discussed and mutually respected. The horizon of each local church was widened therefore because of the great number of possibilities leading to the same results. It was also an exercise in tolerance, as none of these models could prove itself as being preferable to the others.

This multitude of views and practices concern witness or mission not only in non-Christian regions but also among those members of the Orthodox Church who have abandoned God's message. The approach of those brothers and sisters can hardly be the same in a secularized society of the post-industrial era as in a society where free worship and catechism are scarcely tolerated. Furthermore, mission in a semi-industrialized tradition-minded society, where many religious beliefs have their adherents, needs a basically different confrontation. It is unecessary to point out that this polyphony by no means implies a discordance in the theological conception of mission, but simply demonstrates that one and the same reality can appear with various faces.

Furthermore, the unanimity of Eastern and Oriental Orthodox churches was not limited only to purely practical and methodological aspects, but embraced as well the ecclesiological meaning of mission, reflecting the traditional concept of this diakonia among Christians of the east.

The discussion of these problems and the fact that they can receive various realistic and traditionally acceptable solutions is very important and strengthens Orthodox self-consciousness. Each local church realizes in that way that differences in methodology do not affect unanimity in theological and dogmatic questions, and furthermore it becomes aware of the fact that flexibility is necessary when dealing with cultural peculiarities of those receiving God's word to the extent, of course, that the Christian message is not affected by this policy.

This theological unanimity, and the awareness of the existence of various methodological approaches to mission, render the Orthodox churches ready to participate in a constructive discussion with any type of experience western churches would present in San Antonio. In that way the Orthodox presence can be rational, theologically well-founded and practically efficient, holding firmly to the patristic ecclesiology but open to any new methodology. This equilibrium between the traditionally understood ecclesiological dimension of mission and the flexibility in approaching missionary work has been successfully expressed in the final report, rendering this document a valuable tool for the Orthodox churches and an important contribution to the world conference.

Last, but not least, the role of the Parish of the Announciation, who was host the consultation, should be mentioned. The liturgical life of the local congregation was considerably strengthened by the presence of the delegates, and furthermore the living diakonia of the parish and its experience in "internal" mission at the very basic level were important examples of how mission work should be practiced and expanded. Surely this example will not be forgotten by the Orthodox delegation in San Antonio.

Dr Evangelia Varella
Thessaloniki, Greece

Reflections of a silent observer

Over the past thirty-eight years I have attended many consultations on the mission of the church but none like the Consultation of Eastern Orthodox and Oriental Orthodox churches in Neapolis, Greece. This event was characterized by at least four remarkable qualities:

(1) There was an exciting freshness in the composition of the conference. Not in living memory had all but three of the Orthodox churches of the world sent official representatives to reflect together for a week on such a theme as "Your will be done: Orthodoxy in mission."

(2) A clearly focused vision of the whole inhabited earth as the appropriate field for Orthodox witness and service was offered. This vision generated an enthusiastic response from a broad range of laity and clergy. Some of these men and women appeared to be receiving this vision of the world as their parish as a new dimension in their understanding of discipleship. I envied them as I thought of the many Christians for whom the call to global mission is a tiresome, unchallenging topic. I thought of the comparable circumstance when I had observed the eagerness of adults who were reading the gospel for the first time and responding to it as fresh good news in contrast to those who found the gospel to be a much too-familiar lifeless narrative they had heard over and over since childhood.

(3) The call to action issued by the articulate missionaries at the consultation -- bishops, clergy and laity -- was passionate

and powerfully articulate. Their words were credible for they were demonstrably supported by the costly integrity of personal commitment on the part of these women and men at work in places as scattered as Kenya, Alaska, Ghana and Lebanon.

(4) Our hosts in the Parish of the Announciation, Evosmos, Thessaloniki provided us with a case study in contagious faithfulness and community service. The exuberant vitality of this congregation inspired the entire consultation and influenced its work to a degree difficult to exaggerate.

This observer left the consultation moved by many evidences of the working of the Holy Spirit throughout the week. I also carried away two unanswered questions. The first is not likely to appear on the agenda of any future Orthodox consultations; the second, I believe, will command attention one day.

My first question may be typically Protestant. In what way do Orthodox conceive of the celebration of the eucharist to be the very heart of their witness to the world across the centuries when access to this holy feast is closed? That is, how does an event closed to the public provide a public witness?

My second question springs from Protestant experience but, I believe, will need to be addressed by Orthodox before long. How will the Orthodox respond to accusations of proselytism from the existing churches in Africa and Asia if increasing numbers of Methodists, Baptists and Presbyterians become Orthodox in nations where there has been no history of Orthodoxy? Is the Orthodox commitment to global mission a commitment to the extension of Orthodoxy as the one true church throughout the world? Or is there another goal?

I am grateful to have attended this unprecedented event to observe the excitement and joyful acceptance by so many men and women of the challenging call to disciple and nations in response to Christ's command. The next stages of this mission pilgrimage by this venerable, faithful community will be of tremendous significance for the total world Christan community.

Dr Frederick Wilson,
Administrator,
World Conference on Mission and Evangelism

APPENDICES

THE CONTRIBUTORS

H.G. Bishop ANASTASIOS of Androussa,

professor at the University of Athens, director of the "Apostoliki Diakonia" of the Church of Greece, and actually *locum tenens* in the Archbishopric of Eastern Africa (Patriarchate of Alexandria); he is the moderator of the Commission on World Mission and Evangelism, (CWME).

Sister Agapie ASAAD,

from the Daughters of St Mary Coptic Orthodox monastic community; she is a member of the Orthodox Advisory Group, CWME,.

The Rev. Fr Khajah BARSAMIAN,

minister of the Armenian Diocese of North America under the jurisdiction of the Armenian Apostolic Church, Etchmiadzine, USSR; he is presently preparing his doctoral thesis in Rome.

The Rev. Prof. Emmanuel CLAPSIS,

professor of Systematic Theology at the Holy Cross School of Theology, Brookline, MA.

Prof. Olivier CLEMENT,

professor of History at the Saint Serge Institute of Orthodox Theology, Paris, France.

The Rev. Fr Joseph EL-ZAEHLAOUI,

responsible for a community belonging to the Greek Orthodox Patriarchate of Antioch and living in Limassol, Cyprus.

The Rev. Archim. Alexandros KALPAKIDIS,

rector of the Parish of the Announciation in Evosmos, Thessaloniki, and host of the Consultation.

Ms Milia KHODR,

member of the Orthodox Youth Mouvement in Lebanon as well as of the World Student Christian Federation.

Dr Dimitra KOUKOURA,

teacher of Comparative Literature in a public secondary school; she is also involved in catechism and other educational activities of the church.

The Rev. Fr K.M. GEORGE,

senior secretary at the New Delhi office of the National Christian Council of India; he is a member of the Faith and Order Commission.

The Rev. Fr Kwame LABI,

parish priest in Ghana, and an active member of Syndesmos.

H.G. Bishop Antonios MARCOS,

responsible for African Affairs of the Coptic Orthodox Church and secretary of the Organization of African Independent Churches, which has its seat in Nairobi, Kenya.

The Rev. Fr Michael OLEKSA,

pastor in Alaska for many years, at present serves a parish in California; he is member of the WCC Dialogue Sub-Unit Working Group.

Mr Constaninos PAPADAKIS,

teacher of Religious Education in a public secondary school and coordinator of Christian education and youth activities in the Parish of the Announciation in Evosmos, Thessaloniki.

H.G. Bishop STEFAN of Zicha,

former CICARWS commissioner.

The Rev. Archim. Sotirios TRAMBAS,

responsible for the "Orthodox Mission Centre" in Seoul, South Korea.

LIST OF PARTICIPANTS

Church delegates

H.G. ANASTASIOS, Bishop of Androussa, **CWME Moderator**
(Church of Greece)
Athens University, Faculty of Theology, Terma Ano Ilision, Panepistmioupolis,
GR - ATHENS

Rev. Stephanos AVRAMIDES
(Church of Greece)
Ioannou Gennadiou 14, GR - 11521 ATHENS

Rev. Viken AYKAZIAN
(Armenian Apostolic Church, Etchm./USSR)
5, rue Jean-Violette, CH - 1205 GENEVA

H.G. Bishop Amba BISHOY
(Coptic Orthodox Church)
Anba Rueis Building, Ramses St., Abbasiya, P.O. Box 9035,
Nasr City, CAIRO - Egypt

H.G. Archbishop Nerses BOZABALIAN
(Armenian Apostolic Church, Etchm./USSR)
Holy See of Etchmiadzine, Armenian SSR - USSR

H.G. CHRISTOPHOROS
Bishop of Olomouc-Brno (Orthodox Church of Czechoslovakia)
V. Jamé 6, PRAGUE 1 - Czechoslovakia

Rev. Protopr. Haralambos COURRIS
(Church of Cyprus)
Holy Archbishopric of Cyprus, P.O. Box 1130, NICOSIA - Cyprus

Prof. Ivan Zhelev DIMITROV
(Bulgarian Orthodox Church)
4, Oborischte, BG - 1090 SOFIA

Rev.Joseph EL-ZAHLAOUI
(Greek Orthodox Patriarchate of Antioch)
c/o MECC, P.O. Box 4259, LIMASSOL - Cyprus

H.G. Philipose Mar EUSEBIUS, Episcopa
(Malankara Orthodox Syrian Church)
Basil Aramana, Pathanamthitta, KERALA 689645 - India

Rev. Paul Njoroge GATHURU
(Greek Orthodox Patriarchate of Alexandria)
P.O. Box 146, MATATHIA - Kenya

Rev. Dr K.M. GEORGE
(Malankara Orthodox Syrian Church)
Delhi Orthodox Centre, 2, Institutional Area, Tughlagabad,
NEW DELHI 110 062 - India

H.E. Abuna GREGORIOS
Archbishop of Shewa Diocese (Ethiopian Orthodox Church)
P.O. Box 1283, ADDIS ABABA - Ethiopia

Ms Anja HAKONEN
(Orthodox Church of Finland)
Ortodoksinen Lähetes RY, Liisankatu 29, SF - 00170 HELSINKI 17

H.E. IRENEOS
Archbishop of Ierapolis (Greek Orthodox Patriarchate of Jerusalem)
Eretheos 18, GR - 10556 ATHENS

Prof. Vasil ISTAVRIDIS (Ecumenical Patriarchate)
Yeni Yuva Sok. 47/1, Beyoglu-Cihangir, TR - ISTANBUL

Rev. Hieromonk Benedict KANTERS
(Russian Orthodox Church)
Moscow Patriarchate, Danilowsky Val 22, 113191 MOSCOW - USSR

Rev. Kegham KHATCHERIAN
(Armenian Apostolic Church, Cil/Lebanon)
Armenian Church, Dialetti 4, GR - 54621 THESSALONIKI

Mr Elekiya KIHALI
(Greek Orthodox Patriarchate of Alexandria)
P.O. Box 46119, NAIROBI - Kenya

Dr Mikolaj KOZLOWSKI
(Polish Orthodox Church)
Ul. Kutnowska 21, 04.090 WARSAW - Poland

Prof. Christos KRIKONIS
(Church of Greece)
Thessaloniki University, Faculty of Theology, GR - THESSALONIKI

Rev. Archim. Gennadios LIMOURIS
(Greek Orthodox Patriarchate of Alexandria)
WCC, 150, rte de Ferney, CH - 1211 GENEVA 20

H.G. Bishop Antonios MARKOS
(Coptic Orthodox Church)
P.O. Box 21570, NAIROBI - Kenya

Protodeacon Vladimir NAZARKIN
(Russian Orthodox Church)
Moscow Patriarchate, Danilowsky Val 22, 113191 MOSCOW - USSR

Mr Nicolaos NICOLAIDES
(Church of Cyprus)
Holy Archbishopric of Cyprus, P.O. Box 1130, NICOSIA - Cyprus

Rev. Michael OLEKSA
(Orthodox Church in America)
95, Mountain View Ave, Santa Rosa, CA 95407 - USA

Rev. Dirayr PANOSSIAN
(Armenian Apostolic Church, Cil/Lebanon)
c/o MECC, P.O. Box 4259, LIMASSOL - Cyprus

Prof. Constantinos PATELOS
(Greek Orthodox Patriarchate of Alexandria)
Terspsitheas 26, GR - 17563 PALAION PHALIRON

Rev. Radomir RAKIC
(Serbian Orthodox Church)
Ul. 7 Jula nr 5, BELGRADE - Yugoslavia

Dr Ioan SAUCA
(Romanian Orthodox Church)
Institut de Théologie de Sibiu, SIBIU - Romania

H.G. Bishop STEFAN of Zicha
(Serbian Orthodox Church)
Monastery of Zicha, 3600 KRALJEVO - Yugoslavia

Ms Constance TARASAR
(Orthodox Church in America)
St Vladimirs Seminary, 575 Scarsdale Rd, CRESTWOOD, N.Y. 10707 - USA

Rev. Archim. Sotirios TRAMBAS
(Ecumenical Patriarchate)
Akyon dong Mapo ku Seoul, C.P.O. Box 1473, SEOUL - South Korea

Rev. G. Protopr. George TSETSIS
Moderator of the Consultation
(Ecumenical Patriarchate)
WCC, 150, route de Ferney, CH - 1211 GENEVE 20

Prof. Sotirios VARNALIDIS
(Ecumenical Patriarchate)
Doiranis 40, GR - 546 38 THESSALONIKI

Mr Mstislav VOSKRESENSKY
(Russian Orthodox Church)
Moscow Patriarchate, Danilowsky Val 22, 113191 MOSCOW - USSR

Prof. Theodoros ZISSIS
(Church of Greece)
Thessaloniki University, Faculty of Theology, GR - THESSALONIKI

Consultants

Sister Agapie ASAAD, Orthodox Advisory Group
(Coptic Orthodox Church)
The Daughters of St Mary, Box 30, BENI-SOUEF - Egypt

Rev. Khajay BARSAMIAN
(Armenian Apostolic Church, Etchm./USSR)
34, via del Podere Rosa, I - 00137 ROME

Rev. Prof. Emmanuel CLAPSIS
(Ecumenical Patriarchate)
Holy Cross School of Orthodox Theology, 50 Goddard Ave.,
BROOKLINE, Ma 02146 - USA

Prof. Olivier CLEMENT
(Ecumenical Patriarchate)
St Sergius Orthodox Theological Institute, 13, rue de Crimée, F - 75019 PARIS

Rev. Dimitrios COUCHELL, Orthodox Advisory Group
(Ecumenical Patriarchate)
The St Photios Foundation, 41, St George Street, Drawer AF,
ST AUGUSTINE, Fl 32085 - USA

Ms Milia KHODR
(Greek Orthodox Patr. of Antioch)
c/o WSCF Office, P.O. Box 1375, BEIRUT - Lebanon

Dr Dimitra KOUKOURA
(Church of Greece)
37, Vas. Konstantinou, GR - 54622 THESSALONIKI

Deacon Evangelos KOUROUNIS
(Ecumenical Patriarchate)
Greek Orthodox Archdiocese of North and South America,
10 East 79th Street, NEW YORK, NY 10021 - USA

Rev. Kwame LABI, "Syndesmos"
(Greek Orthodox Patriarchate of Alexandria)
P.O. Box 10, LARTEH - Ghana

Rev. Michael G. ROSHAK, NCCC/USA
(Orthodox Church in America)
475 Riverside Drive, NEW YORK, NY 10115 - USA

Rev. Protorp Dragan TERZIC
(Serbian Orthodox Church)
74000 DOBOJ - Yugoslavia

Dr Andreas TYLLIRIDIS
(Greek Orthodox Patriarchate of Alexandria)
P.O.Box 46119, NAIROBI - Kenya

Prof. Christos VANTSOS, Thessaloniki University
(Church of Greece)
University of Thessaloniki, Faculty of Theology, GR - THESSALONIKI

Prof. Petros VASSILIADIS, Thessaloniki University
(Church of Greece)
Thessaloniki University, Faculty of Theology, GR - THESSALONIKI

Mr Milos VESIN
(Serbian Orthodox Church)
Berglistr. 17a, CH - 6005 LUZERN

Observers

Monk ELIAS
Agia Triada, I.M. Hilandar, GR - 63086 MT ATHOS

Mr George KOUKOUTSIDIS
Athanasiou Diakou 8, GR - THESSALONIKI

Rev. Fr. MILINKOVIC
c/o Monastery of Zicha, 3600 KRALJEVO - Yugoslavia

Mr Panaghiotis PAPADIMITRAKOPOULOS
Association for External Mission, 6, Mackenzie King, GR - THESSALONIKI

Mr Magdi SAMUIL
c/o Vlatadon Monastery, Akropolis, GR - THESSALONIKI

Mr Jean TCHEKAN
Service orthodoxe de presse et d'information, 14, rue Victor-Hugo, FR - 92400 COURBEVOIE

Ms Sophie TSO
c/o 8, Vatheos, GR - 115 22 ATHENS

Dr Evangelia VARELLAS
Agn. Stratiotou 1, GR - 54631 THESSALONIKI

Rev. Fr VASSILJEVIC
c/o Monastery of Zicha, 3600 KRALJEVO - Yugoslavia

Local diocese and parish

H.E. Metropolitan DIONYSIOS of Neapolis and Stavroupolis
Rev. Archim. Alexandros KALPAKIDIS

Ms Georgia CHALKIDOU
Ms Anna KARAMANIDOU
Ms Heleni KARAMANIDOU
Ms Maria MAVROMICHALIS
Mr George MILKAS
Ms Georgia MILKAS
Mr Sotirios NICOLAIDES
Mr Ioannis OUSTABASSIDIS

Mr Costantinos PAPADAKIS
Mr George PAPADAKIS
Ms Sophia PAVLIDOU
Ms Despina SAMOLADA
Ms Glykeria SAMOLADA
Mr Antonios SEFERIDIS
Mr Costas SEFERIDIS

WCC Staff

Rev. Prof. Ion BRIA (RCL)
Sister Joan DELANEY,mm (CWME)
Rev. Gueorgui GLOUCHIK (JPIC)
Rev. Heikki HUTTUNEN (YOUTH)
Mr George LEMOPOULOS (CWME)
Ms Annika MAYU (CWME)
Ms Teny PIRRI-SIMONIAN (OICD)
Prof. Todor SABEV (Gen. Sec.)
Rev. Dr Eugene STOCKWELL (CWME)
Rev. Fredrick WILSON (CWME)

" THY WILL BE DONE "
MISSION IN CHRIST'S WAY
FOR ORTHODOXY TODAY *

INTRODUCTION

When he taught us to pray his prayer, the Lord "commanded every one of us who prays to take care of the whole oikoumene, for he did not tell us to pray '*Thy will be done in me or in us*' but '*everywhere on earth*' so that error might be abolished and the truth planted, all evil driven out and the good restored" (St John Chrysostom, PG 57, 279-280).

In the spirit of these words in which the patristic tradition of the universality of salvation is epitomized, the Orthodox Church realizes that in proclaiming the good news of salvation in Christ and acting with commitment in today's tormented and desperate world its mission is to "take care of the whole oikumene."

In the same spirit, the imperative of a constant endeavour to "plant out the truth of the Gospel" and to "drive out all evil" -- the divisions, inequalities and injustices -- demonstrates clearly that everywhere and always the church is -- and must be -- in a missionary situation. The gospel, the good news, is to be spread by Christ's disciples to the ends of the earth and to the end of time.

* This text wich served as a background document, was drafted by members of the Orthodox Advisory Group with the cooperation of several brothers and sisters. Its aim was to indicate some guidelines to Orthodox reflection on the questions raised in the preparatory phase of the world conference (San Antonio) and so facilitate the task of the Orthodox Consultation in Neapolis.

The response to this specific demand of the Lord's Prayer, therefore, can only take the form of an unwearying endeavour to show the world both the will of God and his love and to do so by preaching, teaching, healing, casting out demons and, finally, by the willingness to accept even martyrdom. Every Christian, every member of the body of Christ -- man or woman, young or not so young -- whether clerical or lay, monastic or secular, is called -- in parish, monastery or diocese -- to share in this endeavour and to play an active part in it, to act with commitment in a mission "in Christ's way" so that the will of the heavenly Father may be done in our world today.

Since the primary object of this mission, therefore, is that "the truth be planted," Orthodox Christians have a special responsibility to be witnesses to the "whole truth," to make known this truth that sets people free, this *pleroma* of revelation, this preaching, this apostolic tradition that is the living deposit of the faith, the *parakatatheke*, which has been entrusted to them and to which they have a responsibility to bear witness, with great humility and in spite of all their sins, both to their Christian brothers and sisters and to the whole world.

Our being Orthodox confers on us a very special missionary responsibility. This is not a question of proselytism, i.e., of canvassing for members for this or that local church, but of presenting to the world "the pure image" of Christ so that those who contemplate it may themselves be able to build or complete their own local church. It is a matter of "describing" Christ, not of winning partisans.

I. TURNING TO THE LIVING GOD

a) Conversion -- repentance

"O come, let us worship and bow down before Christ Himself, our King and our God." These are the opening words of the daily liturgical cycle (Office of Vespers).

Thus, drawing on its experience of daily prayer, the church begins its missionary work by summoning each individual to turn towards the living God, to a change (conversion) of heart, sincere repentance and newness of life. This is the church's daily response to Christ's call: "Come, follow Me!" (cf. Matt. 9:9).

Expression can be given to this attitude of the church only in the unbroken search for the will of God. Since, moreover, this will of God is sought in the liturgical sharing of the word, the experience of conversion and repentance are found concretely in the whole of the sacramental life of the community. Thus, drawing on this liturgical treasury, the church invites its members to a collective repentance so that, answering the summons of their Lord who describes the church as "holy and without blemish,...without spot or wrinkle or any such thing" (Eph. 5:27), they may increasingly become identifiable with it. What the church is in virtue of the creative call of its Lord, its members are all to become. The celebration of the eucharist is the supreme moment when the celebrants and the faithful, the whole of the people of God, declare with one voice their repentance and earnestly seek "the grace, mercy and *philanthropia* (love towards humanity) of the One Son" (Liturgy of St John Chrysostom).

Only a community of converts can bear a sincere missionary testimony, and one that is effective. Mission "in Christ's way" presupposes a community of Christians who are "conformed to Christ" not simply because they belong by birth to a confessional social group bearing the label "Christian," but because of a genuine conversion to Christ and a profound repentance both personal and communal. We must now in our daily lives really assume responsibility for what we ourselves, or our godparents as sponsors in our name, proclaimed at our baptism ("I have renounced Satan, all his works and all his pomp," "I cleave to Christ," "I believe in Him as King and as God").

But have we really turned away from these idols of Satan -- from the love of money, the thirst for power, eroticism, chauvinism, racism, partisan passions, etc.? Have we really "turned round," really been converted, so as now to cleave to Christ with complete personal conviction, to approach him, our eyes fixed firmly on the will of the Father, pressing on towards Christ in order to lay hold of him, "straining forward to what lies ahead"? (cf. Phil. 3:12-14). The fact is that our missionary influence depends more on what we really are as individuals and as a church community than on the meticulous organization of our missionary structures. A group of persons that seeks to assert its confessional identity out of a need for social cohesion cannot claim to be the church. Its "religion" is only an alibi for its nationalism or its colonialism. All such a group can do is proselytize. A Christ-bearing community, on the contrary, one that prays to and adores exclusively him who loved us to the point of sacrificing himself for us on the cross is essentially a missionary community. It is by repentance and conversion that the transition is made from the one status to the other. Repentance and conversion then become a decisive element in the life of each believer and in the ecclesial life of each community. By conversion we acquire freedom vis-à-vis the pressures and constraints of society. By repentance we become "conformed to the glorious gospel" (I Tim. 1:11). By repentance we become conformed to the will of God and to the image of his glory (Liturgy of St Basil). It is then that we discover the novelty of the gospel.

b) Witnessing in a secularized world

The repentance of each individual member of the body of Christ is not an attempt to appear just in the sight of others. It is a struggle to acquire qualities of the heart, faith, mercy, justice (Matt. 9:19). The witness that the church is called to bear today in the societies within which it lives is a Christian witness, the testimony of a holy life.

The sometimes exclusive development of scientific reason is the main feature of contemporary civilization. It is often accompanied by a hardness of heart, a loss of human contact, of the human warmth and joyful conviviality that marks off the church of those who have been raised from the dead from the religious association as defined in the laws of our secularized régimes. Mission "in Christ's way" has to bear witness to this "heart of flesh" rekindled by the Spirit of Pentecost and replacing the "heart of stone" of our robotized societies.

These societies have in our time become familiar with the phenomenon of secularization in varying degrees and in more than one form. In this situation, the church's mission consists of showing that this witness, that of a holy life, is necessarily concerned with all aspects of human life: family, society, economy, politics, education, the media, etc. It is a matter of affirming and demonstrating that the separation of the sacred and the secular is unthinkable for the spirit of the gospel. Only in this way will it be possible for each Christian community to demonstrate that the ultimate goal of its mission, even in the midst of difficulties and constraints, is to become an authentic sign of the kingdom of God.

If this is the mission of the church in its entirety, that of theological reflection and ecclesial life will be to arrive at a distinction between the negative forms of secularization (for example, that which tries to diminish the content of faith by asserting the autonomy of earthly values, or that which wants simply to eliminate faith altogether) and a secularization that proves its positive and indispensable character by affirming, in opposition to the semi-totalitarianism of Christianity, the specificity and freedom of the human person, this person who (according to the decision of the Third Preconciliar Pan-Orthodox Conference) has, "as the creature made in the image and likeness of its Creator, constituted for the Orthodox Church the fullness of its mission in the world."

c) The Pentecostal character of the church's mission

Before they go forth "to make disciples of all nations, baptizing them in the name of the Father and of the Son and of the Holy Spirit" (as the Lord commanded them according to the final words of Matthew's gospel), the disciples are told: "Stay in the city until you are clothed with power from on high" (Luke 24:49). Pentecost must come before mission. The disciples will be incapable of doing the will of the Father if they have not first received the Holy Spirit. The unique Spirit will visit them on the day of Pentecost to enable them to proclaim the unique word of God, distributing a diversity of gifts to each of them in a multiplicity of tongues of fire.

There is only one incarnate word, uttered via a multiplicity of tongues.

There is only one Spirit, distributing a multiplicity of gifts.

So too, there is only one apostolic tradition, only one gospel, finding expression through a multiplicity, a diversity, of local cultures.

The good news allows itself to be permeated with the values and riches of each particular culture or, rather, it permeates and transfigures them by the incarnation of the Word. Contemporary secular culture is not to be regarded as any less permeable to the gospel than the pagan culture of ancient Greece evangelized by Paul and his companion, or the societies evangelized by Cyril and Methodius. It contains, perhaps as much as these cultures, some seeds of truth.

But the legitimate and enriching diversity of local traditions (each having received its own gifts) must never be confused with the confessional differences. Diversity must never degenerate into divergence. Here we should heed the words of St Irenaeus:

> Though languages differ throughout the world, the content of the Tradition is one and the same. Neither the churches established in Germania nor those among the Iberians, nor those among the Celts, nor those of the East in Egypt or in Lybia, nor those established at the centre of the world, are of a different Tradition. But just as the sun, this creature of God, is one and the same in all the world, so too this Light which is the proclamation of the Truth shines everywhere and illumines all who wish "to come to the knowledge of the Truth". The most gifted speaker among the heads of the churches will not say otherwise, for no servant is above his Master, nor will the least eloquent diminish this Tradition for, the faith being one and the same, the one who is able to discourse eloquently on it does not have more than this nor the one who says little of it less (*Against the Heresies I*, 10, 2).

Out of this arises the permanent necessity of conciliarity at all levels of the church's life in order that "the unity of the faith and the communion of the Holy Spirit" may be maintained, with due respect for the diversity and individuality of each local church "that the Divine Trinity may be glorified" (Canon 34 of the Apostles).

To maintain unity among the local Orthodox churches -- and also to seek unity with the non-Orthodox churches by a patient effort of witness in the dialogue with them so that they, too, may be able to bring their own gifts to full fruition -- is a missionary imperative. In both cases, the unity maintained or sought has as its purpose the mission "that they may all be one, that the world may believe."

Conversely, however, missionary individuals and communities who bear witness together to their common faith in Christ and proclaim together the same word, find themselves in communion and discover their unity in Christ. If unity makes mission effective, mission leads to unity, not only to the unity of "the holy churches of God," for which we pray in the divine liturgy, but also to the unity of the human race, of "the entire universe," which is the ultimate goal of the church's mission even if a goal only to be fully achieved at the end of time "when all things will be subjected to God" and "the Son himself will be subject to him who subjects all things to him in order that God may be everything to everyone" (I Cor. 15:28).

II. PARTICIPATING IN SUFFERING AND STRUGGLE

a) The eucharistic experience

"Being fed on the body and Blood of the Lord in the Holy eucharist, we experience the need to share God's gifts with our brothers and sisters, we understand better what hunger and deprivation mean and struggle to end them" (decision of the Third Preconciliar Pan-Orthodox Conference).

It is in the eucharistic experience, itself a sharing of the bread of life and the bread of pilgrims, that the idea of sharing and the principle of participation in the struggle and suffering of the neighbour find their fullest expression.

The eucharist, as the sacrament of the altar, becomes the supreme missionary sacrament, since it is by definition the "sacrament of the poor," the sacrament of brothers and sisters. By the dynamic movement that it generates, we enter into this vast unity, we become members one of another, we find ourselves responsible for one another. Each one of us becomes representative of the whole of humanity.

Undoubtedly, therefore, communion in Christ, faith in Christ and the proclamation of Christ as Lord and Saviour are robbed of their meaning if they are separated from the diaconal mission, from the concrete commitment to succour the neighbour, from the effort to share with the neighbour his/her trial and suffering.

The heavy responsibility that falls on the church today, therefore, is to demonstrate concretely both by its action and by its theological reflection that the eucharist is not only a "medicine of immortality" (*pharmakon athanasias*) but must become a "medicine of justice and sanctification" (*pharmakon dikaiosynes kai hagiasmou*) for every gathering that celebrates it and for every individual who participates in it.

b) Power and potentiality -- gifts of God

It is after the sacramental sharing of the gospel message and the body of the Lord that the whole people of God exclaim: "For every good gift and every perfect gift is from above, coming down from Thee, the Father of Lights..." (Liturgy of St John Chrysostom).

We have here, once again, a response by the community to the Lord's promise: "You will be clothed with power from on high" (Luke 24:49). Indeed it is God, the living God, who sends each one of us into the world, who gives unfailingly, and who by his Spirit opens to each one of us an infinite space of power and freedom.

It remains to be seen precisely how each Christian and each Christian community make use of the power granted to them in their everyday life. For it must be confessed in complete sincerity that there are many Christians today who are proud of their spiritual and material riches, their authority, their culture and their intelligence, without realizing -- and so without acknowledging -- that in all these things it is a matter of gifts of God and not of personal accomplishment.

The questions arising from this are searchingly relevant. As Christians, communities or parishes, as local churches, are we following the way of Christ, who himself realized clearly that he had been "given," i.e., had "received" all power on earth and in heaven? Are we following him in his complete self-emptying (*kenosis*) in order to demonstrate that the only legitimate power is that of crucified love? By our testimony and the example of our lives are we demonstrating that God not only gives but also forgives?

Brothers and sisters, entire peoples and nations, are suffering today from a complete lack not only of material blessings but also of power and freedom of action. It is beyond the shadow of a doubt that they need the support of the prophetic voice and the missionary commitment of the church and of every individual Christian.

c) Martyria and martyrion

It being the case that each Christian and the church as a whole bear testimony (*martyria*) by raising their prophetic voice amid the many storms of this world, it is no less true that their authentically Christian commitment can even lead to martyrdom (*martyrion*).

The testimony borne confirms the love and the purpose of God by the proclamation in word and deed of the good news of salvation. The martyr, for his or her part, confirms our human love as an extension of the love of God, a disinterested love, a love that becomes the driving force of our behaviour in the world. Precisely in this way, the martyr confirms fidelity to the will of God. For the martyr is one who accepts every form of final deprivation; the imitator of Christ *par excellence* (cf. Ignatius of Antioch). He or she is the one who is in communion with the Lamb slain, not only sacramentally in the eucharistic mystery but also empirically by his or her joyful acceptance of persecution for righteousness sake.

Martyrdom, however, is not necessarily interpreted in the sense of a physical sacrifice but in the wider sense of a complete readiness for the will of God despite all obstacles, in the sense of a long journey bearing the burden of the cross and the gospel truth, in the sense of a deliberate identification with the most unfortunate end of a sharing of the sufferings and cares of the neighbour.

The indispensable weapon of the church's mission is in fact the cross and not the crusade. A person or community is missionary if they are able to say with St Paul: "I live, yet no longer I but Christ who lives in me" (Gal. 3:20). Such a person or community bears witness, in fact, to the living presence of Christ. In order to arrive here, however, it is necessary first to have put to death the old Adam. Christ manifests himself in the life of a person or community in the measure that this person's or this community's cupidity and egoism have been nailed to the cross. "I have been crucified with Christ that I may live to God" (Gal. 2:19).

The name for this is ascesis. If a tree is to grow it has to be pruned. Evil desires must be crucified so that the life in Christ may be manifest. To be a missionary it is necessary to practice ascesis. The famous Photius understood this when at the request of Cyril and Methodius he sent a group of monks to them to establish a monastery in Moravia. The fact is that monasteries are indispensable in a missionary context. Every monastery has a quiet and discreet missionary vocation for where the risen Christ lives, his Spirit spreads. Mission is the very aroma of the church. If it is to flourish, the parasitic plants must be uprooted.

This is why the church has recognized not only the baptism of blood (martyrdom) but also the baptism of ascesis, which has been equally characteristic of its life and presence in the world.

Its mission today, therefore, will consist of filling this ascetic vision with new content and interpreting boldly both it and the ways in which it relates to solidarity with other members of the body of Christ. Ascesis as voluntary renunciation of everything that could be obtained to the detriment of the neighbour, ascesis as voluntary participation in the sufferings of our brothers and sisters, ascesis as a distancing of ourselves from the powerful of this world -- such ascesis could be a constant confirmation of our dying into Christ in baptism, an existential identification with Christ, a persistent endeavour to obey the will of the Father.

Martyrdom is a combat against those who reject the gospel, against these powers who plot together "against Jesus, how to destroy him" (Mark 3:6). This is a struggle that could define the whole Christian life as a testimony (*martyria*) against the forces of evil.

III. THE EARTH IS THE LORD'S

a) Stewards of creation

"It is Thou, Lord, by whose will all things were brought from non-being into existence. By Thy power, Thou dost uphold the universe. By Thy providence, Thou dost govern the world" (Office of Baptism). Once again it is a liturgical affirmation that removes all doubts as to God's sovereignty over creation, as to the fact that God the Creator, who has himself taken charge of the world, has entrusted the earth to the whole human family "to till and to keep" (Gen. 2:15).

Yet the earth today, more often than not, is in the hands of the violent, the powerful, those who conquer it at sword point or else purchase it for astronomical sums. This simply confirms the terrifying fact of our time, namely, that instead of being genuine stewards of creation, a few economically advantaged men and women, a few economically strong countries and nations, manage and distribute the fruits of creation in a manner that is often criminal, live in a scandalously opulent and wasteful way, and abandon themselves to an arms race that threatens the very existence of our planet. This serves not only to highlight the profound identity crisis of our contemporary world (cf. the decision of the Third Preconciliar Pan-Orthodox Conference) but also the fact that the original act of sin, the rebellion against the will of God and also the offence against his creation, is only perpetuated by our all too often irresponsible attitude.

Since the self-centred possession and administration of the creation are an insult not only to every human being created in God's image and likeness but also to God the Creator himself, who identified himself with humanity, the church's mission today is to affirm that passivity or indifference in face of this reality is equivalent to treachery towards God and an absence of an active faith -- a faith that finds its natural expression in charity towards the neighbour and respect for the creation.

b) Peace and justice

Far from betraying its faith and its tradition by adopting a stance on these problems, the church affirms and updates its faith and tradition. Orthodox doctrine and practice have never accepted either the legitimacy of absolute ownership nor the compulsory community of possessions.

In the exercise of his pastoral mission, St Basil the Great constantly stressed that, basically, there is no difference between someone who corners the riches of creation for his or her own profit and the common thief. For both are actually depriving their brothers and sisters of what was generously bestowed on them by the heavenly Father (Hom. 6 on Luke 12, 16; PG 31, 277-278). The important thing is the recognition of this truth. Everything else -- practical philanthrophy and respect for the creation -- follows quite naturally.

What the church is called to denounce, therefore, is the subordination of justice -- and consequently of truth -- to the interests of an individual or group of individuals. For the selfish use of the material, cultural and spiritual riches of our world not only engenders inequality and injustice but also is a serious threat to peace.

The ecclesial communities are then called to bear their testimony and to help to make injustice a thing of the past, above all, by reminding the world that it is the cross and not the crusade that constitutes the most powerful weapon of the Christian.

c) A sacramental approach to the creation

"Having from Thee that which is Thine, we offer it to Thee in all and for all" (Liturgy of St John Chrysostom). In these words, the community of the faithful acknowledges that it receives everything as a gift from God and that it is called to offer everything back to God's keeping as an offering.

What is not offered in this way cannot be sanctified and transfigured. This, moreover, is why every sacrament is primarily a material offering, sealed by the grace and power of the Spirit received in return.

This vision has left its mark on the theological reflection and sacramental practice of the Orthodox Church through the ages. But the church has to reflect and to act in face of the new realities of our world, for there is undoubtedly a contradiction between the baptismal water sanctified by the Spirit and the water we have polluted through our thoughtlessness and unconcern, between the wine of the eucharist, which is a pledge of life, and the adulterated wine, which poisons because of our hunger for profit, between the oil of anointing, which heals the sicknesses of the body and the soul, and the crude oil, which has become the tool of economic speculation.

To reinforce this sacramental approach to creation, the church established the practice of fasting. This practice, along with that of sharing, is in fact part of the main spiritual and social tradition of the church. In accepting these practices, the church wished to demonstrate not only the importance of charity towards the neighbour but also the care we are called to exercise towards creation and its fruits, and the respect we owe to the earth.

IV. TOWARDS RENEWED COMMUNITIES IN MISSION

a) The resurrection: source of renewal in the church

"Set us all on the right way, confirm us in Thy fear, watch over our life, strengthen our steps...." This is the prayer of the faithful to the Lord after they have been enlightened by the proclamation of the gospel and nourished by the body and blood of the crucified and risen Christ. And the answer granted them coincides with that of the risen Christ sending his disciples into the world to carry out their missionary and prophetic ministry: "Go in peace!" (Liturgy of St John Chrysostom).

By virtue of its paschal character, therefore, the divine liturgy puts the resurrection at the very heart and fount of mission and renewal.

Mission is understood, therefore, as the announcement and actualization of Christ's resurrection, effected in and through the community, itself a "sign" of this economy. It is in celebrating the Lord's Easter at all times and in all places that the church becomes manifest in its existence as people of God. The transmission of the message "Christ is risen" is at once an ecclesial and a personal calling. The church is called to spread throughout the whole earth the gifts and blessings of the risen Lord -- love, pardon, reconciliation, justice and peace. These are the gifts that the church itself has received and continues to receive again and again by the invocation of the Holy Spirit, through whom the kingdom of the Lord is in us and among us.

The resurrection thus becomes the source of the new creation, the new heaven and the new earth. What the church aims at in its missionary vocation is not so much its expansion as its edification and growth as the body of the risen Christ. Renewal and growth can be realized, therefore, only through evangelization and missionary practice. The Christian community acts and develops as it shares its Easter joy with others and extends to them its communion with God.

The nature of the church's mission and renewal are defined by this dynamic of communion. The main lesson to be learned from the missionary tradition of Orthodoxy is that the renewal of Christian life in the church depends on the evangelical commitment of Christians to live the resurrection. Only in the difficult performance of its mission, which embraces all aspects of human life, does the community spread and experience renewal.

b) The "ecumenical vision" of the local community

One of the chief contributions of Orthodox theology to the ecumenical dialogue is in fact its ecclesiological vision or, more precisely, the emphasis it places on the local church and its "catholic," universal dimension. Liturgically and sociologically, the universal church exists only in the reality and experience of the local churches. But the local church cannot turn inwards on itself and be swallowed up in self-sufficiency. It is summoned to fulfil its vocation and perform its mission beyond the frontiers of the parish or diocese. It is thus that we not only arrive at a different understanding of the Christian life as a whole but also discover the new possibilities and dimensions of our own ecclesial life.

When a local church loses its missionary awareness, this can be accounted for by the absence of the experience of "catholicity." The important thing is to develop in time and in space the missionary resources that are already present in the liturgical reality, which is at one and the same time the event of gathering together locally *and* the event of being sent out into the world.

The gospel and with it the eucharist do not simply effect reconciliation, nor is it their sole purpose to gather the people together -- they also constitute a challenge to the conversion of others. The summons of the word, a liturgical call to unity, is at the same time an evangelical summons to conversion.

The exchange of visits between Orthodox parishes and dioceses as well as exchange visits between the Orthodox and members of other confessions could be a reminder to us that we have to conquer this paralyzing confessional, nationalist or ethnic complex that hems us in, and that we cannot achieve our complete catholicity without the others.

c) New forms of mission and new profiles of the missionary community

A number of factors demand the renewal of mission but we dwell here on only two of them. First, as the church seeks to embrace all sorts and conditions of human beings and to identify itself with their needs and concerns, it moves in a variety of different human milieux and social contexts. It therefore finds itself obliged, above all, to recognize the real situations existing where contemporary and authentic experiences of the faith are found. The main place where this richness is discovered and recognized is the local community. The groups formed in each local community, whether welded together by human suffering (disabled, the elderly, etc.) or by concern for social and political conditions and issues (the poor, the young, etc.) or, again, in the form of creative movements (calling for the participation of women in mission, encouraging dialogue with the other religions, etc.), should all influence missionary and pastoral strategy. Listening to what they have to say, making pastoral visits to them, tackling seriously their questions and concerns -- these could be some of the ingredients in a process of recognition, culminating in the gathering together of all these groups in the unique eucharistic assembly, within which they become the church, a missionary church, of which they are then the antennae in the world.

Second, we are witnessing today a large-scale mobilization of Christians who are struggling for justice and in defence of human rights -- the rights of men and women created in the image and likeness of God, for "you are God's temple and God's Spirit dwells in you" and "if anyone destroys God's temple, God will destroy him, for God's temple is holy and that temple you are" (I Cor. 3:16-17). This is why these Christians are actively engaged alongside the poor in their struggle against the rulers of this world, the poor who demand of the church a place where their struggle and their hope can be reflected. While it is true that Orthodox worship has always played an important part in the social struggle of Christians, the challenge remains. The church must avoid any separation whatever between orthodoxy and orthopraxis, for such a separation could lead in the direction of moral heresy. Its mission is to make known that the maintenance of this unity and this balance is precisely that which proves most difficult.

In its own life, the church has latent resources: specifically, its saints and its most active members. It is through the pressure of these that it is called to find a new profile.

d) Towards inter-Orthodox solidarity in the field of mission

For some years there has been an observable desire on the part of the local churches to speak with one voice, to share their experiences and to discover a way of participating in the inter-Orthodox ecumenical and missionary endeavour.

In the face of new needs and with deep respect for all local sensibilities, the local Orthodox churches are working towards a common response. Seeking such solidarity and implementing it in practice are not simply a matter of ecclesiastical strategy but imply the visible exercise of the conciliar spirit among churches that are often isolated and estranged.

Churches today, living in a milieu steeped in the Orthodox tradition, remind their sister churches of the wealth of a centuries-old tradition of spirituality. Those living in a pluralist context stress the importance of dialogue and discussion. Finally, the youngest sister church, one of the newest and smallest of the Orthodox churches, that of Finland, is displaying to the others a striking passion and zeal for external mission, for the sharing of its spiritual and material resources with other peoples and nations.

This demonstrates that the churches form a single body in which the members are in solidarity one with another. They need the others in order that the body may be built up in its fullness by a mission "in Christ's way." Thus the goal of conciliarity as gathering together and of solidarity as sending forth is, in accordance with God's plan and will, to make of all the churches and their nations, of humanity in its entirety, a single large family in Jesus Christ.

Translated from French by the
Language Service of the World Council of Churches